KARATEDO KATA MODEL FOR TEACHING

空手道形教範

第2指定形
新版

クルルンファ	セイサン	カンクウショウ	エンピ
KURURUNFA	SEISAN	KANKUSHO	ENPI

DAINI SHITEIGATA

マツムラローハイ	ニーパイポ	クーシャンクー	ニーセーシー
MATSUMURA ROHAI	NIPAIPO	KUSHANKU	NISESHI

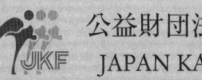

公益財団法人 全日本空手道連盟
JAPAN KARATEDO FEDERATION

カンクウショウ
KANKUSHO

エンピ
ENPI

元衆議院議員
公益財団法人　全日本空手道連盟
会　長　**笹　川　　堯**

序　文

　空手道の稽古に励んで豊かな心と逞しい身体を養い、空手の"道"を通して世界の平和に貢献する皆様と、その指導と発展に情熱を傾ける皆様に心より感謝と敬意を表します。

　1964年に日本全国の空手道を統合しての全日本空手道連盟の誕生以来40年、そして1970年世界空手道連合（現・世界空手連盟）結成以来35年目を迎えます。
　今や空手道は地球のどの国でも普及し、教育やスポーツとして親しまれております。それは空手道が人間育成に有効であることが理解されたからであります。

　人間が平和に生きていくためには、豊かな知識と強い身体と意志が必要であり、そして何よりも平和を愛する心、"人類はみな兄弟姉妹"の心がなければ人類の繁栄はありません。
　空手道の最大の特徴は、
　武器を持たないこと。むやみに攻撃しないこと。そして必勝の信念で身を守ることです。

　空手道は本来、命や財産を守るための武術として発達したものでしたが、現代では外敵から身を守る手段でなく、科学も及ばない病原菌に打ち勝つ体力、そして一人で守るのではなく皆んなで守る協調の精神を養うことを目的とします。
　今後も空手道が現代に生きる武道として、生涯を通じて全世界の人々に愛されるためには、武道の技と心を基盤としたスポーツとして味わいのあるものにしていかなければならないと考えております。
　空手道がさらなる発展を遂げ人類の平和に貢献するためには、強い理念と情熱をもった指導者の育成が必要ですが、そのために空手道の正しい伝統的技術の継承と科学的論理を基盤とする指導書の作成が最も必要と考えます。
　1982年に指定形8つを指定形に制定し、その教本として「空手道形教範」を発行いたしましたが、今回は、新たに8つの指定形を制定し、第2指定形といたし、その教本として「第2指定形・空手道形教範」として発行いたすことになりました。正しい空手道の発展に役立つことを願っております。
　これからも、世界中の皆さんが、生涯にわたって続ける武道スポーツとして親しまれるように、連盟としても一層の努力をしていきたいと思います。

Takashi Sasagawa

Former Member of Representatives
President, Japan Karatedo Federation

Preface

I would like to pay my cordial respect and express my gratitude to all who are diligently developing a sound mind and body by practicing Karatedo (The Way of Karate) and for their passionate guidance and dedicated contribution to world peace through Karatedo.

It has been 40 years since the establishment of the Japan Karatedo Federation, the unified Karatedo of all of Japan, in 1964, and 35 years since the foundation of the World Union of Karatedo Organizations (presently the World Karate Federation) in 1970.

Today, Karatedo has spread all over the world and become very popular in the field of education and sports. This is because Karatedo is considered to be a good means for building character.

It is necessary to have a wealth of knowledge as well as a strong body and mind in order to lead a peaceful life. There is no prosperity for mankind without a love for peace and the belief that "We, humans, are all brothers and sisters."

The prominent characteristic of Karatedo is to protect oneself with the conviction of victory without the use of weapons or reckless attack.

Karatedo was originally developed as a martial art that protects life and fortune. However, today, the objectives of Karatedo are not as a means of defending oneself against outside enemies but the fostering of a spirit of cooperation to defend not by oneself but together with everyone, and the development of physical strength that is resistant to diseases that cannot be cured by medicine.

In order to further the prosperity of Karatedo worldwide as a martial art, a meaningful introduction of the aspects of the sport that are based on the techniques and philosophy behind martial arts will be necessary.

It is essential to publish books that provide guidance that is based on the heritage of accurate traditional techniques and scientific logic so that instructors with solid ideas and enthusiasm can be nurtured. This is also needed to further develop Karatedo and to make a contribution to world peace through Karatedo.

In 1982, a book that described eight designated kata (the sequence of attack and defense techniques) entitled "Karatedo Kata Model for Teaching" was published.

This time, we have selected further eight kata and have published a book on secondary designated kata entitled "Secondary Karatedo Kata Model for Teaching." Our sincere hope is that this book will contribute to promoting the development of true Karatedo.

We are committed to pursue even greater efforts to make Karatedo popular as a martial arts sport that is practiced all over the world for one's entire life.

はじめに

　古来、空手道が武力を養う「武術」として広まり、現代には武力に加え精神力を養う「武道」として発展してまいりました。

　空手道が武道として大きな発展を遂げたことは、素手による攻防で絶妙の動きの中で瞬時に仕留める格闘技としての「組手」の魅力だけでなく、あらゆる攻防の場面を仮想し編成して、余分な技を省き繰り返し励む「形」の両方を練磨するという技術体系によって発展してきました。
　組手により知恵と勇気を養い、形により素朴さと忍耐を養うことにより調和の取れた人間形成を目指すわけです。

　形の繰り返しの修練により、どんな変化にも対応できる俊敏にして強靭な身体と、礼儀を重んじた謙虚な態度となり、なにものにも臆さない精神を養うことで、形の修行が重視されます。
　形は、古来沖縄で空手を伝えた人々によって考案された伝統的な流派の技術の特徴により、重厚堅固を特徴とするものと、敏速軽快を特徴とするものがあります。空手道の技の全てが形に生きており、空手道の特徴は形にあるといって過言でないでしょう。

　全空連では、正しい形の継承と普及のため1982年に8つの指定形を制定し、「空手道形教範」を発行いたしました。各流派に伝統的に継承されている同名の形がありますが、それを一つ選んで全空連指定形として、公式競技会や昇段審査会での演ずることに義務付けました。和道、剛柔、糸東、松濤、四大流派から2つ選出し8つを指定形としました。
　指定形の制定は形の普及に大変役立ち、形が技術的に大きく向上し国内ばかりでなく世界連盟で採用いたすまでになりました。
　さらなる形の普及発展を目指して、今回新たに各会派から2つの形を選出し8つの形を制定し、第2指定形として「第2指定形・空手道形教範」となりました。
　最後になりましたが、本書の発行に携わった方々の絶大なご協力とご苦労に心より感謝を申し上げるとともに、本著の発行がさらなる空手道の発展につながることを祈念して、ご挨拶といたします。

Introduction

Karatedo has been developed as a martial art, which cultivates spiritual strength in addition to a life force known as "martial arts" that was a key element of life in ancient times.

This is a great development for several reasons. In kumite, wisdom and courage is developed through fighting techniques where an unarmed superb performance can instantly determine the outcome of a bout, and at the same time simplicity and perseverance is cultivated through kata training where the essence of the techniques is continuously practiced while envisioning and playing out all parts of a real fight. A well-balanced character is molded through application of both kumite and kata training.

Continuous kata training is considered very important in developing a brave spirit with quick, strong movements that can deal with any changes and a modest attitude with the values of courtesy. The kata handed down in Okinawa is divided into two types: firm, dignified movements and quick, light movements. It is no exaggeration to say that all the techniques and the characteristics of Karatedo can be seen in kata.

In 1982, in order to pass down accurate kata and to encourage their further development, the Japan Karatedo Federation published a book titled "Karate Kata Models for Teaching" consisting of eight kata (two each from the four main styles of Wado, Goju, Shito and Shoto). Each kata is designated by choosing specific ones from several traditionally inherited styles, including kata with common names. The performance of these designated kata is compulsory during official competitions and in exams to graduate to the next belt.

The establishment of designated kata has significantly contributed to the widespread popularization of kata and improvements in techniques not only in Japan but also worldwide. They are now being applied by the World Karate Federation.

We have selected another two kata from each style and are pleased to have reached the publishing stage of a book entitled "Secondary Karate Kata Model for Teaching."

In conclusion, we would like to express our heartfelt appreciation to everyone for their complete cooperation and dedicated efforts in publishing this book.

We sincerely hope that this book will lead to the further development of Karatedo.

CONTENTS
目次

序　文　　笹川　堯

クルルンファ	KURURUNFA	7
セイサン	SEISAN	27
カンクウショウ	KANKUSHO	51
エンピ	ENPI	85
マツムラローハイ	MATSUMURA ROHAI	107
ニーパイポ	NIPAIPO	121
ニーセーシー	NISESHI	147
クーシャンクー	KUSHANKU	165

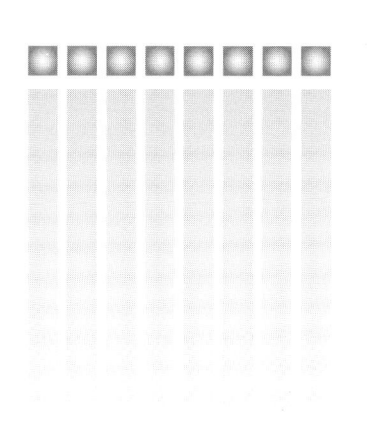

久留頓破
クルルンファ

[特 徴]

この形は、剛柔流の形の中でも開掌を使用した攻防技が多い。
また、動きの速い部分が多く、猫の攻撃の動きのように素早くそしてムチミ（ねばり）のある動きに変わる緩急の動作が特徴である。静から動へのスムーズな変化が要求される。

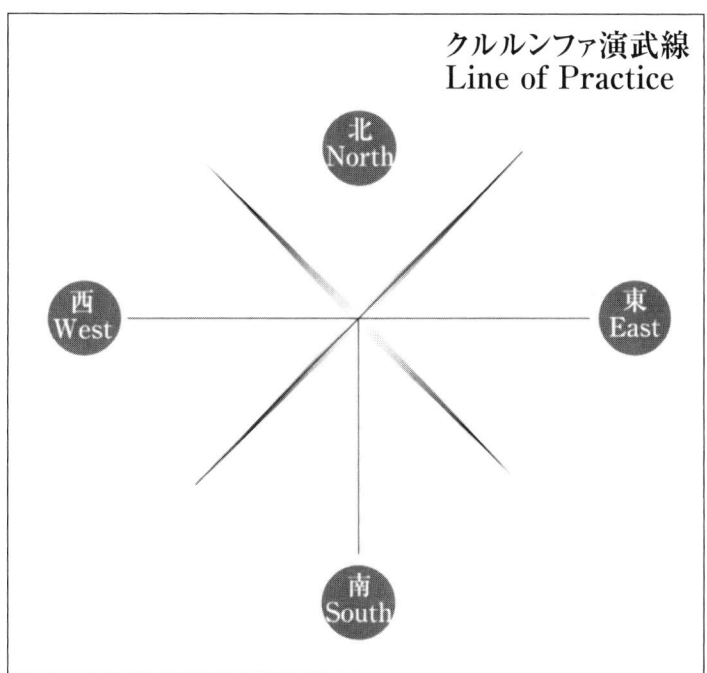

KURURUNFA

[Characteristics]

Of the Goju-Ryu Katas, this Kata has the largest number of defensive and offensive movements using the open palms. It also has many quick movements resembling a cat quick and slow. These movements change speed rapidly. This requires smooth changes from a static to a dynamic state.

クルルンファ

	直立 Stand	用意 Ready	1 挙動 Move	2 挙動 Move
手の動作 Hands	両掌を大腿側部に付け指先を伸ばす。 Open both hands and place both palms on the thighs. Stretch the fingers.	左掌を前にして両掌を交差させ下腹部前に構える。 Place the left palm before the right hand. Cross both palms and hold them in front of the lower abdomen.	両掌を握りながら甲を外にして両体側に構える。 Grasping both hands with the backs of the hands facing outward, hold them along the side of the body.	左肘繰り受け、右掌は小さく押さえながら甲下で水月前。 Execute a Kuri-Uke with the left elbow. Slightly lower the right palm (the back of the hand facing down) and hold it in front of the abdomen.
着眼点 Point to see	南 South	南 South	南 South	南東 Southeast
立ち方 Stance	結び立ち。 Musubidachi	結び立ち。 Musubidachi	平行立ち。 Heikodachi	左猫足立ち。 Left-Nekoashidachi
足の動作 Feet	結び立ち。 Musubidachi	結び立ち。 Musubidachi	上足底を軸に平行立ち。 Pivoting on the toes and Heikodachi. (白から黒へ動く。) (Move from White to Black.)	右足を西に移し左足を寄せて左猫足立ちになる。 Move the right foot towards the west. Pull the left leg and stand in a Left-Nekoashidachi position.
留意点 Point		呼吸は「短呑」。 Breathing: Tandon	呼吸は「長吐」。丹田を中心に全身に力を入れる。 Breathing: Choto. Support the body by exerting force around the navel.	

そのまま。	そのまま。	そのまま。	そのまま。
Maintain the same position.	Maintain the same position.	Maintain the same position.	Maintain the same position.

南東	南東	南東	南東
Southeast	Southeast	Southeast	Southeast

❺	❻	❼	❽

左猫足立ち。
Left-Nekoashidachi

そのまま。		右足を軸に左関節蹴り。	
Maintain the same position.		Pivoting on the right foot, execute a Left-Kansetsu-Keri.	

左膝前の位置を蹴る。
Kick in front of the left knee.

クルルンファ

3 挙 動 Move

手の動作 Hands	右肘繰り受け、左掌は小さく押さえながら甲下で水月前。 Execute a Kuri-Uke with the right elbow. Slightly press down the left palm (the back of the hand facing down) and hold it in front of the abdomen.	そのまま。 Maintain the same position.	そのまま。 Maintain the same position.	
着眼点 Point to see	南東から南西 From southeast to southwest	南西 Southwest	南西 Southwest	南西 Southwest
	❾	❿	⓫	⓬
立ち方 Stance	右猫足立ち。 Right-Nekoashidachi.	右猫足立ち。 Right-Nekoashidachi.		
北 North / 西 West / 東 East / 南 South				
足の動作 Feet	左足刀を戻し、左足を東に移し右足を寄せて右猫足立ち。 Retract the Left-Sokuto. Move the left foot towards the east. Pull the right foot and stand in a Right-Nekoashidachi position.		左足を軸に右関節蹴り、右足刀を左膝近くに引く。 Pivoting on the left foot, execute a Right-Kansetsu-Keri. Pull the Right-Sokuto towards the left knee.	
留意点 Point	猫足の移動の時、上下しない。 Do not bounce the body when you move in a Nekoashi.			

動作の分解 / Kumite in detail

 ①    ②    ③

10

4 挙 動 Move

そのまま。	右掌掬い受け、左掌押さえ受け。	右掌底払い受けの動作、左掌は脇に引く（左掌甲下）。ついで右掌掬い受け、左掌押さえ受け。
Maintain the same position.	Execute a Sukui-Uke with the right palm. The left palm is in an Osae-Uke position.	The movement of a Harai-Uke with the right palm kept downward. Pull the left palm to the side of the body (the back of the hand facing down). At the same time, execute a Sukui-Uke with the right palm. The left palm is in the Osae-Uke position.

南西	南	南（体は東）	南
Southwest	South	South (Body: East)	South

⑬ ⑭ ⑮ ⑯

	右三戦立ち。	半後屈立ち。	右三戦立ち。
	Right-Sanchindachi	Han-Kokutsudachi	Right-Sanchindachi

	右足を前に進め右三戦立ち。	両上足底を軸に左90°転身し半後屈立ち、ついで右三戦立ちに戻る。
	Move the right foot forward and stand in a Right-Sanchindachi position.	Pivoting on both toes, rotate the body to the left 90 degrees and stand in a Han-Kokutsudachi position. Then return to the Right-Sanchindachi position.

	両掌とも中心線にもってくる。	両足の向きを変えるのと腰の捻りを一気にする。
	Move both palms to the center line.	Change the direction of both feet and twist the waist simultaneously.

④ ⑤ ⑥

クルルンファ

	5 挙動 Move	6 挙動 Move
手の動作 Hands	左掌掬い受け。右掌押さえ受け、左掌底払い受けの動作、右掌脇に引く。 Execute a Sukui-Uke with the left palm. The right palm is in the Osae-Uke position. The movement of the Harai-Uke with left palm kept downward. Pull the right palm to the side of the body.	左掌掬い受け、右掌押さえ受け。右掌掬い受け、左掌押さえ受け。 Execute a Sukui-Uke with the left palm. The right palm is in the Osae-Uke position. Then execute a Sukui-Uke with the right palm. The left palm is in the Osae-Uke position.
着眼点 Point to see	南 South　　南（体は西） South (Body: West)	南 South　　南 South
立ち方 Stance	⑰ 左三戦立ち。 Left-Sanchindachi　　⑱ 半後屈立ち。 Han-Kokutsudachi	⑲ 左三戦立ち。 Left-Sanchindachi　　⑳ 右三戦立ち。 Right-Sanchindachi
足の動作 Feet	左足を前に進め、左三戦立ち。両上足底を軸に90°転身し半後屈立ち、ついで左三戦立ちに戻る。 Move the left foot forward and stand in the Left-Sanchindachi position. Pivoting on both toes, rotate the body 90 degrees and stand in the Han-Kokutsudachi position. Then return to the Left-Sanchindachi position.	左三戦立ちから前に進め右三戦立ち。 Moving forward, change the standing position from a Left-Sanchindachi to a Right-Sanchindachi.
留意点 Point		手・足の動作は同時にゆっくり行う。 Move the hands and the feet slowly at the same time.
動作の分解 Kumite in detail		

7 挙 動 Move			
右掌底払い受けの動作、左掌は脇に引く（左掌甲下）。	右掌掬い受け、左掌押さえ受け。	左中段裏受け、右掌は押さえ受け（水月前）。	右掌は小さく押さえ受け、左掌を握りながら。
Execute a Harai-Uke with the bottom of the right palm. Pull the left palm to the side of the body (the back of the hand facing down).	Execute a Sukui-Uke with the right palm. The left palm is in the Osae-Uke position.	Execute a Left-Chudan-Ura-Uke. The right palm is in the Osae-Uke position (in front of the abdomen).	Keeping the right palm in a small Osae-Uke position, grasp the left hand.
南（体は東） South (Body: East)	南 South	南東 Southeast	南東 Southeast
 ㉑	 ㉒	 ㉓	 ㉔
半後屈立ち。 Han-Kokutsudachi	右三戦立ち。 Right-Sanchindachi	左猫足立ち。 Left-Nekoashidachi	左猫足立ち。 Left-Nekoashidachi
		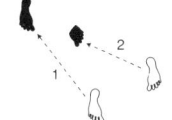	
上足底を軸に左90°転身し半後屈立ち。	右三戦立ちに戻る。	右足を北西に引き、左足を寄せて左猫足立ち。	そのまま。
Pivoting on the toes, rotate the body 90 degrees to the left and stand in a Han-Kokutsudachi position.	Return to the Right-Sanchindachi standing position.	Pull the right foot towards the northwest. Pull the left foot and stand in a Left-Nekoashidachi position.	Maintain the same position.
		左中段裏受けは右掌の外側から受ける。 Receive a Left-Chudan-Ura-Uke at the outer side of the right hand.	

 ⑦  ⑧

クルルンファ

手の動作 Hands	左上段裏突き。 Left-Jodan-Ura-Tsuki	そのまま。 Maintain the same position.	右肘当て。左掌は水月前（甲下）。 Execute a Right-Hijiate. Hold the left palm in front of the abdomen (the back of the hand facing down).	
着眼点 Point to see	南東 Southeast	南東 Southeast	南東（体は北東） Southeast (Body: Northeast)	（北から見る） Seen from the north.
	㉕	㉖	㉗	㉗-A
立ち方 Stance	平行左三戦立ち。 Heiko-Left-Sanchindachi		四股立ち。 Shikodachi	
足の動作 Feet	両足を前に進めて平行左三戦立ち。 Move both feet forward and stand in a Heiko-Left-Sanchindachi position.	右前蹴り。 Execute a Right-Mae-Keri.	右前蹴りから右四股立ち。 From the Right-Mae-Keri, stand in a Right-Shikodachi position.	
留意点 Point	左掌は引かずにその場から握って突く。 Without pulling the left palm, grasp the hand there and execute a Tsuki.		肘当てで気合（肘当ては肩より高すぎないこと）。 When you execute a Hijiate, make a Kiai. (The elbow should not be higher than the shoulder.)	
動作の分解 Kumite in detail	⑨	⑩	⑪	

8 挙動 Move	9 挙動 Move		
両掌を胸前に引き寄せ、左掌上で「天地」に合わせる。 Pull both palms in front of the chest. Place the left palm on top of the right hand. Hold them in the Tenchi position.	右中段裏受け左掌は押さえ受け（水月前）。 Execute a Right-Chudan-Ura-Uke. The left palm is in the Osae-Uke position (in front of the abdomen).	左掌は小さく押さえ受け、右掌は握りながら右上段裏突き。 Keeping the left palm in a small Osae-Uke position, grasp the right hand and execute a Right-Jodan-Ura-Tsuki.	そのまま。 Maintain the same position.
南東から南西 From southeast to southwest	南西 Southwest	南西 Southwest	南西 Southwest
 ㉘	 ㉙	 ㉚	 ㉛
左猫足立ち。 Left-Nekoashidachi	右猫足立ち。 Right-Nekoashidachi	平行右三戦立ち。 Heiko-Right-Sanchindachi	
	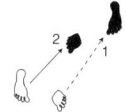	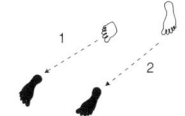	
四股立ちから右足を北西に引き、左足を引き寄せて左猫足立ち。 From the Shikodachi, pull the right foot toward northwest. Pull the left foot and stand in a Left-Nekoashidachi position.	左足を北東に移し、右足を引き寄せて右猫足立ち。 Move the left foot towards the northeast. Pull the right foot and stand in a Right-Nekoashidachi position.	右足から両足をすり足で進めて平行右三戦立ち。 Move both feet forward into a Suriashi, stepping the right foot first and stand in a Heiko-Right-Sanchindachi position.	左前蹴り。 Execute a Left-Mae-Keri.

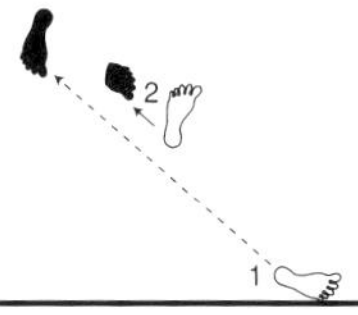

「天地」とは両掌部を向かい合わせた形をいう。

The Tenchi refers to the form in which the both palms are positioned to face each other.

クルルンファ

10 挙 動　Move

手の動作 / Hands

左肘当て。右掌は水月前（甲下）。両掌を胸前に引き寄せ右掌上の「天地」の構え。

Execute a Left-Hijiate. Hold the right palm in front of the abdomen (the back of the hand facing down). Then pull both hands to the front of the chest. Hold them in the Tenchi position, placing the right palm above the left palm.

		右回し受け。	両掌底当て（左掌上）。
		Execute a Right-Mawashi-Uke.	Execute a Ryo-Shotei-Ate.(the left hand stays up)

着眼点 / Point to see

南西 Southwest	南西 Southwest	南 South	南 South
㉜	㉝	㉞	㉟

立ち方 / Stance

| 四股立ち。 Shikodachi | 右猫足立ち。 Right-Nekoashidachi | 右猫足立ち。 Right-Nekoashidachi | 右猫足立ち。 Right-Nekoashidachi |

北 North / 西 West — 東 East / 南 South

足の動作 / Feet

左前蹴りから南西に左四股立ち。左足を北東に引き右足を寄せ右猫足立ち。

Lower the left foot (Left-Mae-Keri) in the southwest direction and stand in a Left-Shikodachi position. Pull the left foot towards the northeast. Pull the right foot and stand in a Right-Nekoashidachi position.

右足を南に移し右猫足立ち。

Move the right foot towards the south and stand in a Right-Nekoashidachi position.

そのまま。
Maintain the same position.

留意点 / Point

肘当てで気合を入れる。
When you execute a Hijiate, make a Kiai.

動作の分解 / Kumite in detail

16

11 挙　動　Move

左裏掛け受け。右掌甲下で脇に引く。

Execute a Left-Ura-Kake-Uke. Pull the right palm (the back of the hand facing down) to the side of the body.

両掌を握り左拳は甲上で胸前、右後ろ肘当て。

Grasp both hands. Turn the left fist so that the back of the hand faces up. Execute a Right-Ushiro-Hijiate to the front of the chest.

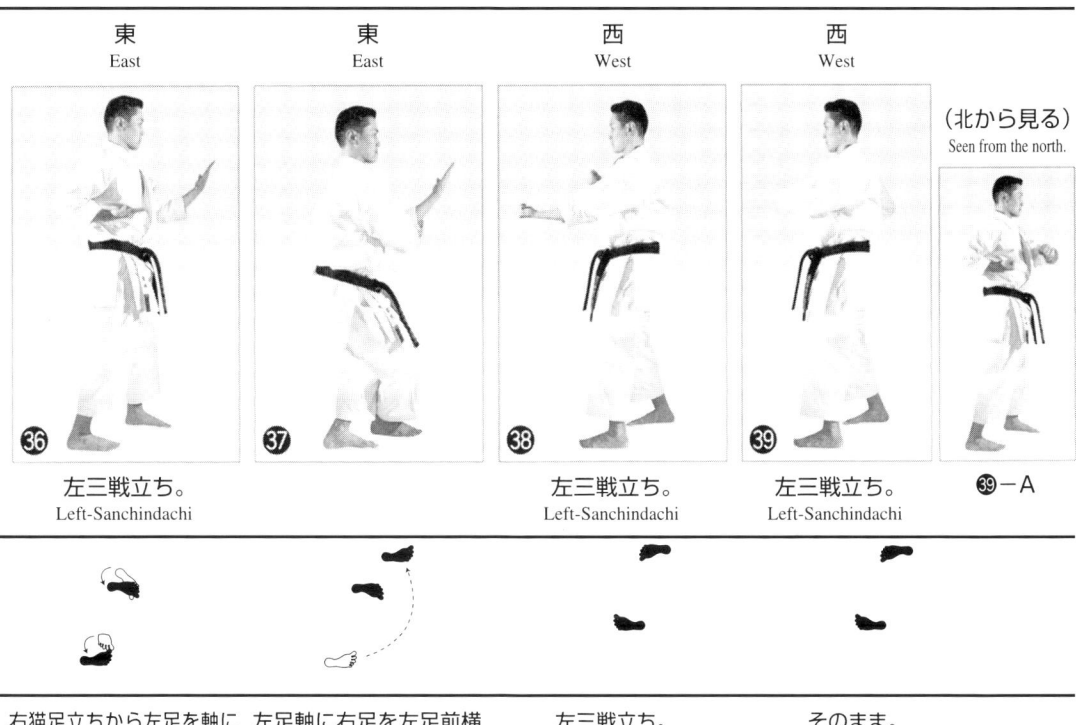

東 East	東 East	西 West	西 West	（北から見る） Seen from the north.
㊱	㊲	㊳	㊴	㊴-A
左三戦立ち。 Left-Sanchindachi	左三戦立ち。 Left-Sanchindachi	左三戦立ち。 Left-Sanchindachi	左三戦立ち。 Left-Sanchindachi	

右猫足立ちから左足を軸に東に90°回転。左三戦立ち。

From the Right-Nekoashidachi position, pivoting on the left foot, rotate 90 degrees to the east. Left-Sanchindachi.

左足軸に右足を左足前横に移しながら西に180°回転。

Pivoting on the left foot and while shifting the right foot to the front and side of the left foot, rotate 180 degrees to the west.

左三戦立ち。

Left-Sanchindachi.

そのまま。

Maintain the same position.

⑫

⑬

⑭

クルルンファ

12 挙 動 Move

手の動作 Hands

右裏掛け受け。左掌甲下で脇に引く。

Execute a Right-Ura-Kake-Uke. Pull the left palm (the back of the hand facing down) to the side of the body.

両掌を握り右拳は甲上で胸前、左後ろ肘当て。

Grip both hands. Hold the right fist (the back of the hand facing up) in front of the chest and execute a Left-Ushiro-Hijiate.

着眼点 Point to see

西 West	西から東 East from West	東 East	（北から見る） Seen from the north.
㊵	㊶	㊷	㊷－A

立ち方 Stance

| 右三戦立ち。 Right-Sanchindachi | 右三戦立ち。 Right-Sanchindachi | 右三戦立ち。 Right-Sanchindachi | |

足の動作 Feet

右足を前に進めて右三戦立ち。

Move the right foot forward and stand in a Right-Sanchindachi position.

右足軸に左足を右足前横に送りながら東に180°回転、右三戦立ち。

Pivoting on the right foot, move the left foot to the front and side of the right foot, then turn the body 180 degrees towards the east, and stand in a Right-Sanchindachi position.

そのまま。

Maintain the same position.

留意点 Point

動作の分解 Kumite in detail

13 挙 動 Move

両掌を右掌上で「二の字」に構える。	両掌を甲上で肩よりやや高く左右に伸ばす。	両肘を軸に前腕を垂直に曲げる。	両掌を合わせ（顔は下方に向ける）。
Hold both hands (palms) (the right hand is on the left hand) in the "Ninoji" position.	Turn both hands so that the backs are facing up. Extend and raise the arms to the side just above shoulder height.	Pivoting on both elbows, raise the forearms vertically.	Hold both hands together. (The face is looking down.)

東から南	南	南	南
South from East	South	South	South
 ㊸	 ㊹	 ㊺	 ㊻
四股立ち。 Shikodachi			

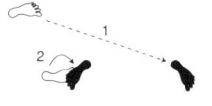			
右足を軸に左足を東に移し四股立ち。	四股立ちから膝を伸ばした姿勢になる。	そのまま。	そのまま。
Pivoting on the right foot, move the left foot towards the east and stand in a Shikodachi position.	In this position, the knees are raised and extended in the Shikodachi standing position.	Maintain the same position.	Maintain the same position.
両掌とも甲上で上下に揃えた形を「二の字」という。			
Placing one palm on the top of the other (the backs of the hands facing up) is called the "Ninoji" position.			

⑮

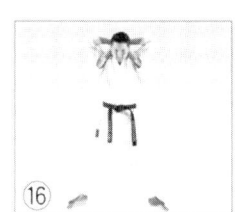
⑯

クルルンファ

手の動作 Hands	両掌の甲を合わせながら頭上に伸ばす（顔は下方に向ける）。 Hold the backs of both hands together above the head and extend them upward. (The face is looking down.)	両肘を内に締め固める。 Hold the elbows tightly together (inward).	両掌底押さえ受け（左掌上）。 Execute a Ryo-Shotei-Osae-Uke. (The left palm is on the right hand.)
着眼点 Point to see	南 South ㊼	南 South ㊽	南 South ㊾
立ち方 Stance		四股立ち。 Shikodachi	四股立ち。 Shikodachi
北 North 西 West ― 東 East 南 South			
足の動作 Feet	そのまま。 Maintain the same position.	素早く腰を落とし四股立ちになる（同時に上を向き後頭部で当てる）。 Quickly lower the waist and stand in a Shikodachi position. (At the same time, turn the head up and hit the opponent with the back of the head.)	そのまま。 Maintain the same position.
留意点 Point	両掌は後頭部を通りながら頭上に伸ばし、両掌の甲を合わせる。 Extend the hands up behind the head and hold the backs of the hands together.	両前腕を合わせると同時に後頭部で当てる。 When you hold the forearms together, simultaneously hit the opponent with the back of the head.	
動作の分解 Kumite in detail		⑰	⑱

20

14 挙動 Move

両掌底を外に張り出したまま両掌を左右に開き、すり上げながら上段交差受け。

Jutting out both palms with its bottom facing outward, pull both hands apart and execute a Jodan-Kosa-Uke by sliding the arms up.

両掌底をすり合わせながら、拳に変えて頭上に連ねる。

Place both palm bottoms together and hold them above the head (center).

南 South	南 South	南 South	南から北 North from South
			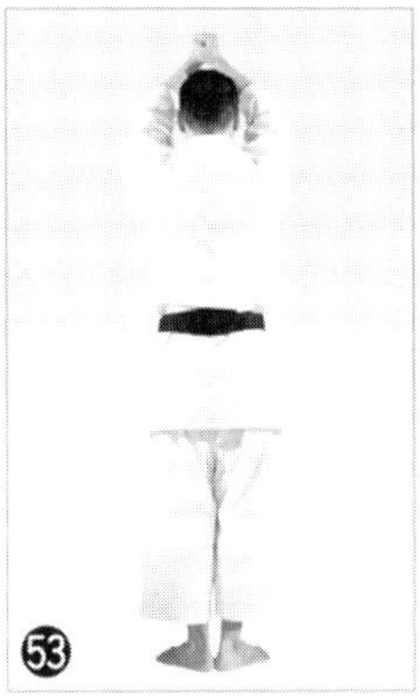
右前屈立ち。 Right-Zenkutsudachi	右前屈立ち。 Right-Zenkutsudachi	右前屈立ち。 Right-Zenkutsudachi	結び立ち。 Musubidachi
			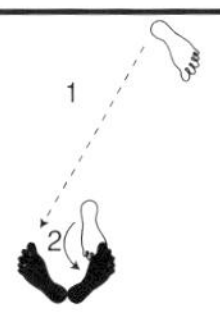
右足を前に出し右前屈立ち。 Move the right foot forward and stand in a Right-Zenkutsudachi position.	そのまま。 Maintain the same position.	そのまま。 Maintain the same position.	右足に左足を引き寄せ右足軸に北方向に180°回転、結び立ち。 Pull the left foot to the right foot. Pivoting on the right foot, rotate the body 180 degrees towards the north and stand in a Musubidachi position.
	交差受けは両掌甲で挟むように受ける。 Receive the Kosa-Uke by pinching it with the backs of the hands.		握った左拳の親指側に右拳を連ねる。 Place the right fist on the thumb side of the grasped left fist.

			⑮ 挙 動 Move	
手の動作 Hands	両拳を連ねたまま振りおろす。 Holding the both fists together, shake the hands down.		右掌を右膝前に出し左掌は甲外で脇に引く。 Push out the right palm in front of the right knee. Pull the left palm (the back of the hand facing outward) to the side of the body.	右掌でかい込み、左掌底当て。 With a scooping motion (Kaikomi), move the right palm up and execute a Left-Shotei-Ate.
着眼点 Point to see	北 North  54	（北から見る） Seen from the north. 	北東 Northeast  55	北東 Northeast  56
立ち方 Stance	爪先立ち。 Tsumasakidachi	54－A	やや深い右前屈立ち。 Deeper Right-Zenkutsudachi	やや深い右前屈立ち。 Deeper Right-Zenkutsudachi
北 North / 西 West / 東 East / 南 South				
足の動作 Feet	結び立ちから爪先立ち。 From a Musubidachi position stand in a Tsumasakidachi position.		左足を軸に素早く右足を北東に出し右前屈立ち。 Pivoting on the left foot, quickly move the right foot towards the northeast and stand in the Right-Zenkutsudachi.	そのまま。 Maintain the same position.
留意点 Point				右掌のかい込みは前腕中ほどまで（かい込みすぎない）。 The scooping motion (Kaikomi) should stop in the middle of the forearms (not to scoop all the way to the end).
動作の分解 Kumite in detail	 23	 24	 25	

16 挙動 Move

左掌を左膝前に出し右掌は甲外で脇に引く。	左掌でかい込み、右掌底当て。	左回し受け。
Jut out the left palm before the left knee, pull the right palm (the back of the hand facing outside) to the side of the body.	With a scooping motion (Kaikomi), move the left palm and execute a Right Shotei-Ate.	Execute a Left-Mawashi-Uke.

（北から見る） Seen from the north.	北東から北西 Northwest from Northeast	北西 Northwest	南 South
		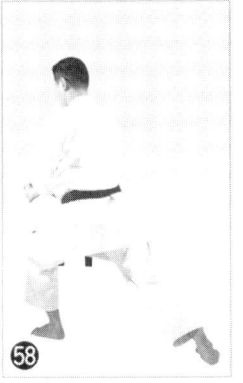	
㊻－A	やや深い左前屈立ち。 Deeper Left-Zenkutsudachi	やや深い左前屈立ち。 Deeper Left-Zenkutsudachi	左猫足立ち。 Left-Nekoashidachi
			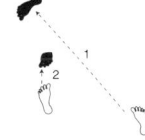
	右足を軸に素早く左足を北西に出し左前屈立ち。 Pivoting on the right foot, quickly move the left foot towards the northwest and stand in a Left-Zenkutsudachi position.	そのまま。 Maintain the same position.	右足を左足の前に進め左に１３５°回転し、左足を引き寄せ左猫足立ち。 Move the right foot to the front of the left foot. Rotate the body 135 degrees to the left. Pull the left foot and stand in a Left-Nekoashidachi position.
		左掌のかい込みは前腕中ほどまで（かい込みすぎない）。 The scooping motion (Kaikomi) should stop in the middle of the forearms (not to scoop all the way to the end).	

クルルンファ

			17 挙 動 Move	18 挙 動 Move
手の動作 Hands	左回し受け。 Execute a Left-Mawashi-Uke.	両掌底当て（右掌上）。 Execute a Ryo-Shotei-Ate. (The right palm is upper.)	右掌を左掌に重ねる（右掌上）。 Place the right hand (palm) on the left hand. (The right hand is on the left hand.)	手前に回しながら下腹部前に構える（左掌前）。 Turn the hands towards you and hold them in front of the lower abdomen. (The left hand is before the right hand.)
着眼点 Point to see	南 South	南 South	南 South	南 South
立ち方 Stance	左猫足立ち。 Left-Nekoashidachi	左猫足立ち。 Left-Nekoashidachi	左猫足立ち。 Left-Nekoashidachi	結び立ち。 Musubidachi
足の動作 Feet	そのまま。 Maintain the same position.	そのまま。 Maintain the same position.	そのまま。 Maintain the same position.	左足を引いて結び立ち。 Pull the left foot and stand in a Musubidachi position.
留意点 Point		両掌ともできるだけ正面に向ける。 Hold both palms facing towards the front as much as possible.		

直　立　Stand

両掌を大腿側部に静かに
戻す。

Open both hands and stretch them down quietly along the thighs. Stretch the fingers.

南
South

結び立ち。
Musubidachi

そのまま。
Maintain the same position.

十三手
セイサン

[特　徴]

　この形は、実戦的、護身的な技の体系と鍛錬動作、剛と柔、動と静が巧みに調和されている形である。
　豪快な突き、蹴りと素早いすり足、蛇のように相手の腕に巻きついての掴み技など変化に富んだ技が含まれている。喉に対する攻撃、開掌による連続受け、蹴りからの連続手技、前蹴りから踵落としと、連続技に富んでいる形である。

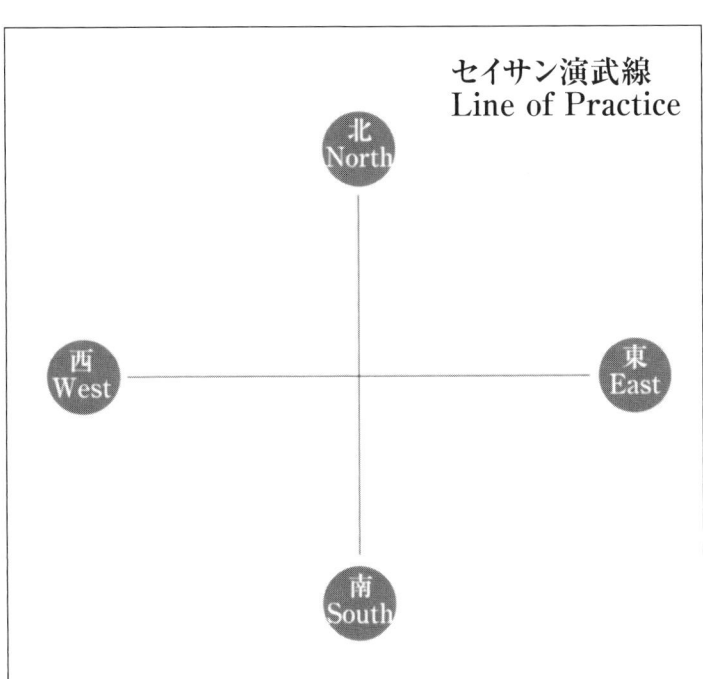

セイサン演武線
Line of Practice

北 North
西 West
東 East
南 South

SEISAN

[Characteristics]

This is a Kata that combines practical and self-defensive wazas, training movements, power and gentleness, and static and dynamic states. It includes diversified wazas such as dynamic jabs (Tsuki), kicks (Keri), quick foot movements (Suriashi), grabbing (Tsukamiwaza) by holding an opponent's hands (like snake coiling). It also contains various continuous wazas such as attacks to the throat, continuous Uke with open palms, continuous hand wazas by kicking (Keri), front kicking (Mae-Keri) and heel drops (Kakato-Otoshi).

セイサン

	直立 Stand	用意 Ready	1 挙動 Move	2 挙動 Move
手の動作 Hands	両掌を大腿側部に付け指先を伸ばす。 Open both hands and place both palms on the thighs. Stretch the fingers.	左掌を前にして両掌を交差させ下腹部前に構える。 Place the left palm before the right hand. Cross both palms and hold them in front of the lower abdomen.	両掌を握りながら甲を外にして両体側に構える。 Grasping both hands with the backs of the hands facing outward, hold them along the side of the body.	両腕を交差させ（右腕外）三戦の構え。 Cross both arms (right arm facing outward), and hold a Sanchin-no-Kamae position.
着眼点 Point to see	南 South	南 South	南 South	南 South
立ち方 Stance	結び立ち。 Musubidachi	結び立ち。 Musubidachi	平行立ち。 Heikodachi	右三戦立ち。 Right-Sanchindachi
北 North / 西 West / 東 East / 南 South			（白から黒へ動く。） (Move from White to Black.)	
足の動作 Feet	結び立ち。 Musubidachi	結び立ち。 Musubidachi	上足底を軸に平行立ち。 Pivoting on the toes and Heikodachi.	右足は弧を描いて進み、右三戦立ち。 Move the right foot forward drawing an arc and stand in a Right-Sanchindachi.
留意点 Point		呼吸は「短呑」。 Breathing: Tandon	呼吸は「長吐」。丹田を中心に力を入れる。 Breathing: Choto. Support the body by exerting force around the navel.	

3 挙動 Move

左拳をゆっくり引き、左中段突き。	三戦の構えに戻す。	三戦の構え。	
Slowly pull the left fist and execute a Left-Chudan-Tsuki.	Return the hands to the Sanchin-no-Kamae position.	Sanchin-no-Kamae	

南	南	南	南
South	South	South	South
❺	❻	❼	❽
右三戦立ち。	右三戦立ち。	右三戦立ち。	左三戦立ち。
Right-Sanchindachi	Right-Sanchindachi	Right-Sanchindachi	Left-Sanchindachi

そのまま。	そのまま。	そのまま。	左足は弧を描いて進み、左三戦立ち。
Maintain the same position.	Maintain the same position.	Maintain the same position.	Move the left foot forward drawing an arc and stand in a Left-Sanchindachi.

中段突きから三戦の構えに戻す動作は一挙動で素早く行う。

Quickly return from the Chudan-Tsuki position to the Sanchin-no-Kamae position in one movement.

セイサン

4 挙動 Move

手の動作 Hands	右拳をゆっくり引いて右中段突き。 Slowly pull the right fist and execute a Right-Chudan-Tsuki.	三戦の構えに戻す。 Return to the Sanchin-no-Kamae.		三戦の構え。 Sanchin-no-Kamae
着眼点 Point to see	南 South ❾	南 South ❿	南 South ⓫	南 South ⓬
立ち方 Stance	左三戦立ち。 Left-Sanchindachi.	左三戦立ち。 Left-Sanchindachi.	左三戦立ち。 Left-Sanchindachi.	右三戦立ち。 Right-Sanchindachi.
北 North / 西 West — 東 East / 南 South				
足の動作 Feet	そのまま。 Maintain the same position.	そのまま。 Maintain the same position.	そのまま。 Maintain the same position.	右足は弧を描いて進み、右三戦立ち。 Move the right foot forward drawing an arc and stand in a Right-Sanchindachi.
留意点 Point		中段突きから三戦の構えに戻す動作は一挙動で素早く行う。 Quickly return from the Chudan-Tsuki position to the Sanchin-no-Kamae position in one movement.		
動作の分解 Kumite in detail				

5 挙 動　Move

左拳をゆっくり引いて左中段突き（突いた拳はそのまま）。	胸前で左掌に右手刀を打ち当てる。	すり上げながら左掌斜め掌底当て、右掌は水月前（押さえ受け）。	
Slowly pull the left fist and execute a Left-Chudan-Tsuki. (Hold the fist at the Tsuki position.)	Execute (hit) a Right-Shuto to the left palm in front of the chest.	Sliding the left palm upward, execute a Left-Shotei-Ate askew. Hold the right palm in front of the abdomen(Osae-Uke).	

南 South	南 South	南 South	南 South
⑬	⑭	⑮	⑯
右三戦立ち。 Right-Sanchindachi	右三戦立ち。 Right-Sanchindachi	右三戦立ち。 Right-Sanchindachi	右三戦立ち。 Right-Sanchindachi

そのまま。	そのまま。	そのまま。	そのまま。
Maintain the same position.	Maintain the same position.	Maintain the same position.	Maintain the same position.

掌底当ては斜めにして顔面下部に掌底当て。

Hold the bottom of the palm facing forward and hit the lower part of the opponent's face with the bottom of the palm.

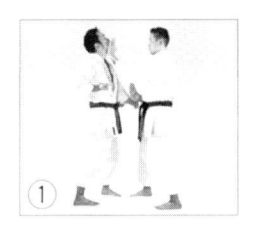

①

セイサン

			6 挙 動 Move
手の動作 Hands	ついで右斜め掌底当て、左掌水月前（押さえ受け）。 Then, slide the right palm upward. The palm should be facing forward. Hold the left palm in front of the abdomen.	左斜め掌底当て、右掌押さえ受け。 Hold the bottom of the left palm up and hold the right palm in the Osae-Uke position.	両掌を素早く返す。 Retract both hands quickly.
着眼点 Point to see	南 South ⑰	南 South ⑱	南 South ⑲
立ち方 Stance	右三戦立ち。 Right-Sanchindachi.	右三戦立ち。 Right-Sanchindachi.	
北 North 西 West ― 東 East 南 South			
足の動作 Feet	そのまま。 Maintain the same position.	そのまま。 Maintain the same position.	右踵が臀部に当たるように、かい込みすり足で前進。 Bend the right leg backward, touching the heel to the hip, move the feet forward into a Suriashi.
留意点 Point		掌底当ては3回連続して行う。 Hit (Shotei-Ate) the opponent three times continuously.	両掌を返す時、両肘が体から離れないように注意し臀部へのかい込みと同時に行う。 When you retract the hands, make sure that both elbows do not move away from the body; at the same time, bend the right leg backward, touching the heel to the hip.
動作の分解 Kumite in detail		②	③

両掌甲上に返し張り突き（稲妻の高さ）。	両掌を素早く返す。	両掌甲上に返し張り突き。
Turn the palms so that the backs of the hands face up and hold them in the Hari-Tsuki position. (to a height of Inazuma)	Quickly turn both palms.	Turn the palms so that the backs of the hands face up and hold them in the Hari-Tsuki position.

南	南	南
South	South	South

⑳ ㉑ ㉒

平行右三戦立ち。	右踵が臀部に当たるように、かい込みすり足で前進。	平行右三戦立ち。
Heiko-Right-Sanchindachi	Bend the right leg backward, touching the heel to the hip, move the feet forward into a Suriashi.	Heiko-Right-Sanchindachi

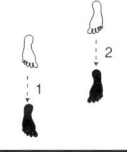

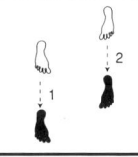

両掌の間は拳一つの間隔で腕は弓張り。手と足の動作は同時にゆっくりと粘り強く行う。	張り突きの動作は3回行う。
Hold the hands (palms) apart so a fist could be inserted between them. Hold the arms in the Yumi-Hari position. Move the hands and feet slowly, simultaneously and consistently.	Repeat Hari-Tsuki three times.

④

セイサン

7 挙 動 Move

手の動作 Hands

両掌を素早く返す。 Turn over both palms quickly.	両掌甲上に返し張り突き。 Turn the palms so that the backs of the hands face up and hold them in a Hari-Tsuki position.	張り突きを握り締めながらゆっくり脇に引く（甲下）。 Grasping the fists, slowly retract the arms (Hari-Tsuki) to the sides of the body. (The back of the hands face down.)	そのまま。 Maintain the same position.

着眼点 Point to see

南 South	南 South	南 South	南 South
㉓	㉔	㉕	㉖

立ち方 Stance

| | 平行右三戦立ち。
Heiko-Right-Sanchindachi | 平行右三戦立ち。
Heiko-Right-Sanchindachi | |

方位: 北 North / 西 West / 東 East / 南 South

足の動作 Feet

| 右踵が臀部に当たるように、かい込みすり足で前進。

Bend the right leg backward, touching the heel to the hip, move the feet forward into a Suriashi. | 平行右三戦立ち。
Heiko-Right-Sanchindachi | 平行右三戦立ち。
Heiko-Right-Sanchindachi | |

留意点 Point

動作の分解 Kumite in detail

⑤

34

そのまま。	そのまま。	左掌底当て、右掌底押さえ受け。
Maintain the same position.	Maintain the same position.	Push out the bottom of the left palm. The bottom of the right palm is in the Osae-Uke position.

南
South

南
South

南から北
From south to north

（北から見る）
Seen from the north.

㉗ ㉘ ㉙ ㉙-A

左三戦立ち。
Left-Sanchindachi

右足関節蹴り（右膝前）。	蹴りの後、左足を軸に北に１８０°回転、左三戦立ち。
Execute a Right-Kansetsu-Keri. (The right knee is in front.)	After the kick, pivoting on the left foot and turn 180 degrees towards the north, and then Left-Sanchindachi.

	左掌底当てはゆっくり粘り強く行う。
	Execute a Left-Shotei-Ate slowly in a tenacious manner.

⑥ ⑦

セイサン

8 挙動 Move

手の動作 / Hands:

右掌掬い裏掛け受けから掌を返して掛け押さえ、左掌底押さえ受け。

From the position where the bottom of the right palm is in the Sukui-Ura-Kake-Uke position, turn the palm and hold it in the Kake-Osae position. The bottom of the left palm is in the Osae-Uke position.

着眼点 / Point to see: 北 / North

㉚

（北から見る）
Seen from the north.

㉚-A

（㉚〜㉛への動作）
Movement of ㉚〜㉛.

立ち方 / Stance:

右三戦立ち。
Right-Sanchindachi.

足の動作 / Feet:

右足を前に進め右三戦立ち。
Move the right foot forward and stand in a Right-Sanchindachi position.

留意点 / Point:

左掌底当てはゆっくり粘り強く行う。
Execute a Left-Shotei-Ate slowly in a tenacious manner.

9 挙動 Move

手の動作 / Hands:

左掌掬い裏掛け受けから掌を返して掛け押さえ、右掌底押さえ受け。

From the position where the bottom of the left palm is in the Sukui-Ura-Kake-Uke position, turn the left palm and hold it in the Kake-Osae position. The bottom of the right palm is in the Osae-Uke position.

着眼点 / Point to see: 北 / North

㉛

立ち方 / Stance:

左三戦立ち。
Left-Sanchindachi.

足の動作 / Feet:

左足を前に進め左三戦立ち。
Move the left foot forward and stand in a Left-Sanchindachi position.

36

10 挙 動 Move

右掌掬い裏掛け受けから掌を返して掛け押さえ、左掌底押さえ受け。

From the position where the bottom of the right palm is in the Sukui-Ura-Kake-Uke position, turn the palm and hold it in the Kake-Osae positon. The bottom of the left palm is in the Osae-Uke position.

北
North

（北から見る）
Seen from the north.

（㉛〜㉜への動作）
Movement of ㉛〜㉜.

（北から見る）
Seen from the north.

㉛ー A

㉜

右三戦立ち。
Right-Sanchindachi

㉜ー A

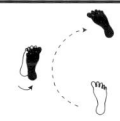

右足を前に進め右三戦立ち。

Move the right foot forward and stand in a Right-Sanchindachi position.

セイサン

11 挙 動 Move

手の動作 Hands	左掌掬い裏掛け受け右掌底押さえ受け。 The bottom of the left palm is in the Sukui-Ura-Kake-Uke position. The bottom of the right palm is in the Osae-Uke position.		
着眼点 Point to see	北 North	北 North	
	(㉜～㉝への動作) Movement of ㉜～㉝.	㉝	(北から見る) Seen from the north. ㉝-A	㉞
立ち方 Stance		左三戦立ち。 Left-Sanchindachi		左三戦立ち。 Left-Sanchindachi
北 North / 西 West / 東 East / 南 South				
足の動作 Feet		左足を前に進め左三戦立ち。 Move the left foot forward and stand in a Left-Sanchindachi position.		そのまま。 Maintain the same position.
留意点 Point		掬い裏掛け受けの動作は計4回行う。 Repeat the Sukui-Ura-Kake-Uke movement four times.		
動作の分解 Kumite in detail				⑧

38

12 挙 動 Move

左掌掬い裏掛け受けから左掌を返しながら握って脇に引く（甲下）。

From the position where the bottom of the left palm is in the Sukui-Ura-Kake-Uke position, grasp the left hand, turn it up and retract it to the side of the body. (The back of the hand faces down.)

右掌は掛け受けから螺旋を描きながら五指を握り締める。

Whirling the right hand, grasp fingers from Kake-Uke to clench fist.

北から東
From north to east

東
East

東
East

（北から見る）
Seen from the north.

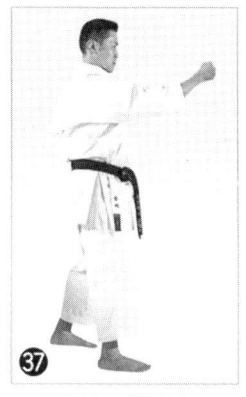

㉟ ㊱ ㊲ ㊲-A

左三戦立ちから平行右三戦立ち。
From Left-Sanchindachi to Heiko-Right-Sanchindachi.

平行右三戦立ち。
Heiko-Right-Sanchindachi

平行右三戦立ち。
Heiko-Right-Sanchindachi

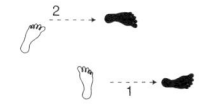

両上足底を軸に東に向きを変えながら、右足から前に進めて平行右三戦立ち。

Turning to the east by pivoting on both feet, move the right foot forward and stand in a Heiko-Right-Sanchindachi position.

そのまま。

Maintain the same position.

そのまま。

Maintain the same position.

右掌握り締めの位置は喉の高さ。

Grasp the right hand at the throat.

⑨  ⑩  ⑪

39

セイサン

13 挙動 Move

手の動作 Hands	左中段突き。右拳は脇に引く。 Execute a Left-Chudan-Tsuki. Pull the right fist to the side of the body.	右中段突き。左拳は脇に引く。 Execute a Right-Chudan-Tsuki. Pull the left fist to the side of the body.	右中段突き。左拳は脇に引く。右腕をやや押さえながら脇を締める。 Execute a Right-Chudan-Tsuki. Pull the left fist and retain it under the shoulder joint. Lower the right arm a little and keep it close to the side.	そのまま。 Maintain the same position.
着眼点 Point to see	東 East ㊳	東 East ㊴	東 East ㊵	東 East ㊶
立ち方 Stance	平行右三戦立ち。 Heiko-Right-Sanchindachi	平行右三戦立ち。 Heiko-Right-Sanchindachi	平行右三戦立ち。 Heiko-Right-Sanchindachi	
北 North 西—東 West—East 南 South				
足の動作 Feet	そのまま。 Maintain the same position.	そのまま。 Maintain the same position.	そのまま。 Maintain the same position.	右足を上げ、左足片足立ちとなる。 Raise the right foot and stand on the left foot.
留意点 Point	左右中段突きは連続して行う。 Execute a Left/Right Chudan-Tsuki continuously.			
動作の分解 Kumite in detail				

14 挙　動　Move

そのまま。	左掌底当て右掌底押さえ受け。	左掌掛け受け右掌脇（甲上）。	右中段突き（甲上のまま受けた方向を突く）、左拳脇に引く。
Maintain the same position.	Push out the bottom of the left palm. The bottom of the right palm is in the Osae-Uke position.	Execute a Kake-Uke with the left palm. Pull the right palm to the side of the body (the back of the hand facing up).	Execute a Right-Chudan-Tsuki. (The back of the hand faces up; execute a Tsuki.) Pull the left fist to the side of the body.
東 East	東から西 From east to west	西 West	西 West
 ㊷	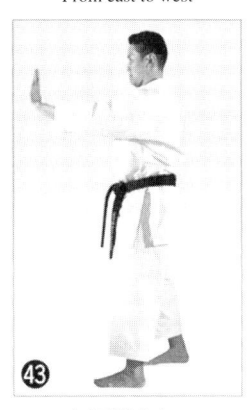 ㊸	 ㊹	 ㊺
	左三戦立ち。 Left-Sanchindachi	左四股立ち。 Left-Shikodachi	左四股立ち。 Left-Shikodachi
右足関節蹴り。	 左足を軸に180°回転し西向き左三戦立ち。	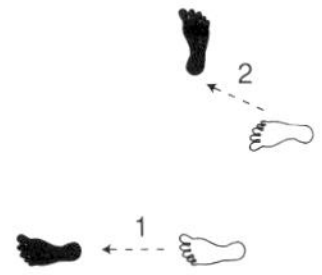 左足から前に進み左四股立ち。	 そのまま。
Execute a Kansetsu-Keri with the right foot.	Pivoting on the left foot, turn 180 degrees towards west, and stand in a Left-Sanchindachi position.	Move the left foot forward and stand in a Left-Shikodachi position.	Maintain the same position.
関節蹴りは右膝前の位置を蹴る。	左掌底当ては素早く行う。	足と手の動作は素早く行う。	
Kick (Kansetsu-Keri) the opponent in the right shin.	Quickly push out the bottom of the left palm.	Move the hands and feet quickly.	

⑫　⑬

41

セイサン

15 挙　動　Move

手の動作 Hands	左中段突き。右拳は脇に引く。 Execute a Left-Chudan-Tsuki. Pull the right fist to the side of the body.	右中段突き。左拳は脇に引く。 Execute a Right-Chudan-Tsuki. Pull the left fist to the side of the body.	右腕でやや押さえながら脇を締める。 Press down the right arm slightly to the side of the body, leaving no space under the shoulder joint.
着眼点 Point to see	西 West	西 West	西 West
	㊻	㊼	㊽
立ち方 Stance	左四股立ち。 Left-Shikodachi	左四股立ち。 Left-Shikodachi	左四股立ち。 Left-Shikodachi
北 North / 西 West / 東 East / 南 South			
足の動作 Feet	そのまま。 Maintain the same position.	そのまま。 Maintain the same position.	そのまま。 Maintain the same position.
留意点 Point			右左右の3連続突き。 Execute a Tsuki three times continuously in Right-Left-Right combination.
動作の分解 Kumite in detail	⑭	⑮	⑯

そのまま。

Maintain the same position.

そのまま。

Maintain the same position.

右拳上げ突き左掌押さえ受け（水月前）。

Execute an Age-Tsuki with the right fist. The left palm is in the Osae-Uke position (in front of the abdomen).

西

West

㊾

西

West

㊿

西から北

From west to north

(51)

（北から見る）

Seen from the north.

(51)−A

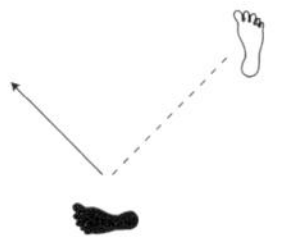

左足軸に右足を引き寄せ北西に右関節蹴り。

Pivoting on the left foot, pull the right foot and execute a Right-Kansetsu-Keri towards the northwest.

四股立ちからの関節蹴りは左軸足膝が伸びきらないよう注意する。

When executing a Kansetsu-Keri from the Shikodachi position, make sure you do not fully extend the knee on the left leg (pivoting).

気合を入れる。

Make a Kiai.

⑰

セイサン

手の動作 Hands	右上段裏拳打ちから肘落とし。左掌水月前。 Execute a Hiji-Otoshi from a Right-Jodan-Uraken-Uchi. Hold the left palm in front of the abodomen.	
着眼点 Point to see	北 North	（北から見る） Seen from the north. （52〜53への動作を北から見る） Movement of 52〜53 seen from the north.
立ち方 Stance	四股立ち。 Shikodachi	52-A
北 North / 西 West 東 East / 南 South		
足の動作 Feet	蹴った足を引いて北におろし四股立ち。 Pull and lower the leg (kicked) to the floor and stand in a Shikodachi position.	そのまま。 Maintain the same position.
留意点 Point		
動作の分解 Kumite in detail		⑱ ⑲ ⑳

44

16 挙動 Move		17 挙動 Move
右拳払い受け。左掌水月前。 Execute a Harai-Uke with the right fist. Hold the left palm in front of the abdomen.	左掌を拳にして甲上の寸突き、右拳は脇に引く。 Grasp the left hand and execute a Sun-Tsuki with the back of the hand facing up. Pull the right fist to the side of the body.	そのまま。 Maintain the same position.

(52〜53への動作を北から見る)
Movement of 52〜53 seen from the north.

北
North

53

四股立ち。
Shikodachi

(北から見る)
Seen from the north.

53-A

北
North

54

そのまま。 Maintain the same position.	そのまま。 Maintain the same position.	左足軸に右足を引き寄せ右関節蹴り。 Pivoting on the left foot, pull the right leg and execute a Right-Kansetsu-Keri.
	左拳は水月前から突く。 Execute a Tsuki with the left fist from the front of the abdomen.	左軸足は伸びきらないこと。 Do not fully extend the left foot (pivoting).

㉑ ㉒

45

セイサン

18 挙動 Move

手の動作 / Hands

そのまま。 Maintain the same position.	左掌掛け受けから右掌を胸前で行き合わせる。 From the Kake-Uke position, push the right palm out to the front of the chest with the left palm.	両掌を握りながら拳を返し、脇に引く（甲下）。 Grasp both hands, turn them up and pull them to the side of the body. (The back of the hand facing down).

着眼点 / Point to see

北 North	北から南 From north to south	南 South	南 South
㊻	㊺	㊼	㊽

立ち方 / Stance

| | 左三戦立ち。
Left-Sanchindachi | 左三戦立ち。
Left-Sanchindachi | 左三戦立ち。
Left-Sanchindachi |

北 North / 西 West / 東 East / 南 South

足の動作 / Feet

| | 左足を軸に南方向に90°回転し左三戦立ち。
Pivoting on the left foot, rotate the body 90 degrees towards the south and stand in a Left-Sanchindachi position. | そのまま。
Maintain the same position. | そのまま。
Maintain the same position. |

留意点 / Point

動作の分解 / Kumite in detail

㉓ ㉔

46

19 挙動 Move

そのまま。	右正拳突き。（肩の高さ）左掬い流し受けをしながら左掌を上腕基部に添える。	左回し受け。
Maintain the same position.	Execute a Right-Shoken-Tsuki (shoulder height). Execute a Left-Sukui-Nagashi-Uke, place the left palm at the base of the upper arm.	Execute a Left-Mawashi-Uke.

南	南	南
South	South	South

�59 ㊱60 ㊱61

	左半前屈立ち。	左猫足立ち。
	Left-Han-Zenkutsudachi	Left-Nekoashidachi

右足は前蹴りから膝を曲げぬように引き（踵落とし、着地）左半前屈立ち。		右足軸に左足を引き寄せ左猫足立ち。
After a Mae-Keri, pull the right leg without bending the knee (dropping the heel (Kakato-Otoshi) and landing), stand in a Left-Han-Zenkutsudachi position.		Pivoting on the right foot, pull the left foot and stand in a Left-Nekoashidachi position.

気合を入れる。
Make a Kiai.

㉕ ㉖ ㉗

セイサン

			20 挙動 Move	**21** 挙動 Move
手の動作 Hands	左回し受け。 Execute a Left-Mawashi-Uke.	両掌底当て（右掌上）。 Execute a Ryo-Shotei-Ate. (The right palm is upper.)	右掌を左掌に重ねる（右掌上）。 Place the right hand (palm) on the left hand. (The right hand is on the left hand.)	手前に回しながら下腹部前に構える（左掌前）。 Turn the hands towards you and hold them in front of the lower abdomen. (The left hand is before the right hand.)
着眼点 Point to see	南 South ㉒	南 South ㉓	南 South ㉔	南 South ㉕
立ち方 Stance	左猫足立ち。 Left-Nekoashidachi	左猫足立ち。 Left-Nekoashidachi	左猫足立ち。 Left-Nekoashidachi	結び立ち。 Musubidachi
北 North 西 West ― 東 East 南 South				
足の動作 Feet	そのまま。 Maintain the same position.	そのまま。 Maintain the same position.	そのまま。 Maintain the same position.	左足を引いて結び立ち。 Pull the left foot and stand in a Musubidachi position.
留意点 Point		両掌ともできるだけ正面に向ける。 Hold both palms facing towards the front as much as possible.		

直 立 Stand

両掌を大腿側部に静かに
戻す。

Open both hands and stretch them down quietly along the thighs. Stretch the fingers.

南
South

㊿

結び立ち。
Musubidachi

そのまま。

Maintain the same position.

観空小
カンクウショウ

[特　徴]

観空大と同様の敵を仮想しての技の編成であるが、棒の受けと反撃に特徴がある。上段の棒受け、掴み捻って押し込む。さらに脛を払う棒攻撃に、膝をかい込み高く飛び上がり、一回転して反撃をかわす。最後も三日月蹴りから一回転して伏せて攻撃をかわし、鋭い中段突きで仕留めて終わる。松濤館流の中で最も敏速果敢な形といわれる。

KANKUSHO

[Characteristics]

This Kata constitutes the wazas assuming the same enemy as for Kankudai but this kata has special offense and defense characteristics using the pole. In this waza, the player grabs the pole from Jodan and twists and pushes it back. When the attacker tries to hit the shin with the pole, the player jumps high, bending the knees, and fends off the attack by rotating the body once. In the end, the player executes a Mikazuki-Keri, and fends off the attack by rotating the body once and crouching on the floor. At the end, the player executes a quick Chudan-Tsuki to the opponent. This Kata is said to be the most quick and brave kata in Shotokan-Ryu.

カンクウショウ

	直立 Stand	用意 Ready	**1** 挙動 Move
手の動作 Hands	両手は開いて大腿部両側に付けて伸ばす。 Open both hands and stretch the arms down to the sides of the thighs.	両拳大腿部前（両拳甲前向き）。 Both fists are in front of the thighs. (The backs of the fists face forward.)	両拳同時に動かして、左中段諸手受け。右拳は小指側を左肘内側に添える。 Moving both fists simultaneously, execute a Left-Chudan-Morote-Uke. Place the right fist (little finger) on the inside of the left elbow.
着眼点 Point to see	南 South	南 South	東 East
立ち方 Stance	結び立ち。 Musubidachi	八字立ち。 Hachijidachi	右後屈立ち。 Right-Kokutsudachi
北 North 西 West ― 東 East 南 South		（白から黒へ動く。） (Move from White to Black.)	
足の動作 Feet	結び立ち。 Musubidachi	結び立ちから八字立ち。 Hachijidachi from Musubidachi	右足を半歩西へすり出す。 Slide the right foot for a half-step to the west.
留意点 Point			中段諸手受けは、肘の角度を保ち、高く上がらないように注意。 In executing Chudan-Morote-Uke, make sure that the elbow stays at a right angle. Do not raise it too high.

(2〜3への動作)
Movement from 2 to 3.

2 挙動 Move	**3** 挙動 Move
両拳同時に動かして右中段諸手受け、左拳は小指側を右肘内側に添える。 Moving both fists simultaneously, execute a Right-Chudan-Morote-Uke. Place the left fist (little finger) on the inside of the right elbow.	両拳同時に動かして左中段諸手受け、右拳は小指側を左肘内側に添える。 Moving both fists simultaneously, execute a Left-Chudan-Morote-Uke. Place the right fist (little finger) to the inside of the left elbow.

西
West

南
South

(❸〜❹への動作)
Movement from ❸ to ❹.

(❹〜❺への動作)
Movement from ❹ to ❺.

左後屈立ち。
Left-Kokutsudachi

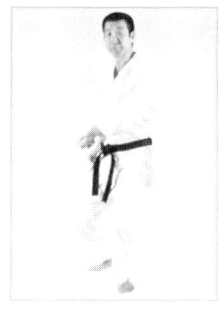

右後屈立ち。
Right-Kokutsudachi

| 右脚を軸として、東へ左足をすり出す（寄足）。

Pivoting on the right foot, slide the left foot towards the east (Yoriashi). | 右足を北へすり出す（寄足）。

Slide the right foot towards the north (Yoriashi). |

［備考］寄足で左側方へ。

[Note] Move towards the left in a Yoriashi.

カンクウショウ

	4 挙動 Ⓐ　Move Ⓐ	**4 挙動 Ⓑ　Move Ⓑ**
手の動作 Hands	右中段順突き。左拳左腰に引く（甲下向）。 Execute a Right-Chudan-Jun-Tsuki. Pull the left fist to the left waist. (The back of the hand faces down).	右手首を掴まれたので右前腕を外転し、外す（甲下向）。 The opponent has grabbed the right wrist. Release by twisting the right forearm outward. (The back of the hand faces down.)
着眼点 Point to see	南　South　（西から見る）Seen from the west.	南　South　（西から見る）Seen from the west.
立ち方 Stance	右前屈立ち。 Right-Zenkutsudachi	右前屈立ち。 Right-Zenkutsudachi
足の動作 Feet	左脚を軸として、右足を南へ進める。 Pivoting on the left foot, move the right foot towards the south.	立ち方はそのまま。 Maintain the same standing position.
留意点 Point	［備考］4-ⒶⒷを一挙動で敏速に行う。 [Note] Quickly execute 4-Ⓐ and Ⓑ simultaneously.	［備考］突いた瞬間に肘の力を抜いて、前腕を外転し脇を強く締める。肘は受けではないから曲げすぎない。 [Note] The moment you execute a Tuski, relax the elbow, twist the forearm outward and hold the elbow tightly against the side. Since the elbow is not in a Uke, do not bend it too much.
動作の分解 Kumite in detail	掴まれた右手首を強く引きながら手首を返す。突いた瞬間に肘の力を抜いて手首を返す。 Turn the wrist by pulling the grabbed wrist (right wrist) towards the body. At the moment the strike is executed, release all the strength from the elbow and turn the wrist.	

5 挙動 Ⓐ　Move Ⓐ

左中段順突き。右拳右腰に引く（甲下向）。

Execute a Left-Chudan-Jun-Tsuki. Pull the right fist to the right waist. (The back of the hand faces down.)

南
South

⑧

左前屈立ち。
Left-Zenkutsudachi

（東から見る）
Seen from the east.

⑧-A

右脚を軸として、左足を南へ進める。

Pivoting on the right foot, move the left foot towards the south.

［備考］ 5-ⒶⒷを一挙動で敏速に行う。

[Note] Quickly execute 5-Ⓐ and Ⓑ simultaneously.

5 挙動 Ⓑ　Move Ⓑ

左手首を掴まれたので左前腕を外転し、外す（甲下向）。

Since the left wrist has been grabbed by the opponent, rotate the left forearm outward and free the left wrist. (The back of the hand faces down.)

南
South

⑨

左前屈立ち。
Left-Zenkutsudachi

（西から見る）
Seen from the west.

⑨-A

立ち方はそのまま。

Maintain the same standing position.

［備考］ 4挙動と同じく。

[Note] Same as Movement 4.

カンクウショウ

6 挙 動 Move

手の動作 / Hands

右中段順突き。左拳左腰に引く（甲下向）。

Execute a Right-Chudan-Jun-Tsuki. Pull the left fist to the left waist. (The back of the hand faces down.)

着眼点 / Point to see

南
South

（西から見る）
Seen from the west.

⑩〜⑪への動作）
Movement from ⑩ to ⑪.

⑩-A

立ち方 / Stance

右前屈立ち。
Right-Zenkutsudachi

北 North / 西 West / 東 East / 南 South

足の動作 / Feet

左脚を軸として右足を南へ進める。

Pivoting on the left foot, move the right foot towards the south.

留意点 / Point

気合。
Kiai.

動作の分解 / Kumite in detail

56

7 挙　動　Move	8 挙　動　Move
右掌中段掴み受け。左掌右手首上添え手。両拳開掌、左肘の下から右掌で円を描き、左掌は右手首を上から添えて右掌中段掴み受け。左掌右手首上添え手。 Execute a Chudan-Tsukami-Uke with the right palm. Place the left palm on the right wrist. Open both hands. Move the right palm from beneath the left elbow, drawing a circle. Place the right wrist on the left palm, and execute a Chudan-Tsukami-Uke with the right palm. Place the left palm on the right wrist.	両手引き寄せ、左手を添えたまま右手を握り、右肘を右脇へ強く引きつける（甲上向）。 Pull both hands and grasp the right hand (the left hand should be touching the right hand). Firmly pull the right elbow to the right side of the body. (The back of the hand faces up.)
北 North	北 North
（西から見る） Seen from the west.	（西から見る） Seen from the west.
⑪　左前屈立ち（逆半身）。 Left-Zenkutsudachi (Gyaku-Hanmi)	⑫　左脚立ち。 Stand on the left foot.
⑪-A	⑫-A
右脚を軸として腰を左へ回転し、左足を北へ進める。 Pivoting on the right foot, rotate the waist to the left and move the left foot to the north.	左足の位置はそのまま、右中段前蹴り（上足底）。 Maintain the left foot position. Execute a Right-Chudan-Mae-Keri (Josokutei).
［備考］ややゆっくり力を込めて、両肘と両脇を強く締める。左掌は拇指を離さないで四指共に付けて添え手とする。 [Note] Slowly exert force. Pull both elbows tightly to the sides. Place the left palm on the right hand while keeping the fingers together.	7 挙動でゆっくり受けた後は、8・9挙動は敏速に行う（⑯・⑰挙動も同じく）。 In Movement 7, protect yourself from the opponent's attack slowly. But, in Movements 8 and 9, act quickly. (Act quickly also in Movements ⑯ and ⑰.)

相手の右中段突きを、腰を左に捻り逆半身になりながら、右拳を開き、左肘下から円を描き物を掴むように受け、左掌は右手首を上から掴むように引き寄せる。

①  ②

When defending an opponent's Right-Chudan-Tsuki, turn the waist to the left (Gyaku-Hanmi), open the right fist, and move the right hand from the underside of the left elbow (drawing a circle). Grab the opponent's Right-Chudan-Tsuki with the right palm and, at the same time, pull the right wrist towards your body with the left palm (the left hand is holding the right wrist from the top).

カンクウショウ

9 挙動 Move

手の動作 / Hands

右裏拳上段縦回し打ち。
左拳は左腰に引く。

Execute a Right-Uraken-Jyodan-Tate-Mawashi-Uchi. Pull the left fist to the left waist.

着眼点 / Point to see

（⑫～⑬への動作）
Movement from ⑫ to ⑬.

北
North

⑬

（西から見る）
Seen from the west.

⑬－A

立ち方 / Stance

右足前交差立ち。
Right-Mae-Kosadachi

```
北 North
西 West ― 東 East
南 South
```

足の動作 / Feet

右足を北へ一歩飛び込み、左足を右踵の後ろに引きつける。

Jump up and place the right foot one step towards the north, pulling the left foot behind the right ankle.

留意点 / Point

交差立ちは、右足に左足をしっかり引きつけ正確堅固な交差立ちとなる。左掌は相手を掴み引きつけるように握り左腰に引き、右拳は左拳を追うように胸前から、顔の前に半円を描くように裏拳打ち。

When you stand in a Kosadachi, pull the left leg to the right foot; then firmly and precisely stand in a Kosadachi. Grab the opponent with the left palm and pull the opponent to the left side of the waist. Execute a Uraken-Uchi with the right fist by moving the right fist from the front of the chest following the left fist, drawing a semi-circle in front of your face.

10 挙 動　Move

右中段外受け。左拳は左腰に引く。

Execute a Right-Chudan-Soto-Uke. Pull the left fist to the left waist.

右前屈立ち（半身）。
Right-Zenkutsudachi (Hanmi)

⑭-A

右足の位置はそのまま、左足を南へ引く。右前屈立ち。

Maintain the right foot position. Pull the left foot towards the south and stand in a Right-Zenkutsudachi position.

11 挙 動　Move

左中段逆突き。右拳は右腰に引く。

Execute a Left-Chudan-Gyaku-Tsuki. Pull the right fist to the right waist.

右前屈立ち。
Right-Zenkutsudachi

⑮-A

立ち方はそのまま。

Maintain the same standing position.

北 / North
（西から見る）/ Seen from the west.

カンクウショウ

	12 挙 動 Move	**13** 挙 動 Move
手の動作 Hands	右中段順突き。左拳は左腰に引く。 Execute a Right-Chudan-Jun-Tsuki. Pull the left fist to the left waist.	右中段外受け。左下段受け。右拳を左腰前に（甲上向）左拳前を右肩前に（甲外向）。右拳は左腰前より右肩の前へ（甲右向）肘を直角に曲げる。左拳は右肩前より脇腹の前。両拳同時に動かす。 Execute a Right-Chudan-Soto-Uke. Execute a Left-Gedan-Uke. Place the right fist in front of the left waist (the back of the hand facing up). Place the left fist in front of the right shoulder (the back of the hand facing out). Move the right fist to the front of the right shoulder from the front of the left waist (the back of the hand facing to the right). Bend the elbow vertically. Move the left fist to the front of the flank from the front of the right shoulder. Move both fists simultaneously.
着眼点 Point to see	北 North	南 South
立ち方 Stance	右前屈立ち。 Right-Zenkutsudachi	右後屈立ち。 Right-Kokutsudachi
足の動作 Feet	立ち方はそのまま。 Maintain the standing position.	右脚を軸とし腰を左へ回転し、左足を南へ進める。 Pivoting on the right foot, rotate the waist to the left. Move the left foot towards the south.
留意点 Point	［備考］挙動 **11**・**12** は敏速に続けて連突き。 [Note] In Movements **11** and **12**, execute a Tsuki quickly and continuously.	［備考］右脚を軸として外受け。下段受けを同時に行う。 [Note] Pivoting on the right foot, execute a Soto-Uke and Gedan-Uke simultaneously.
動作の分解 Kumite in detail		右中段突きを左下段受け ① Execute a Left-Gedan-Uke against the opponent's Right-Chudan-Tsuki.

60

14 挙　動　Move

左表拳振りおろし打ち。
右拳は右腰に引く。

Execute a Furi-Oroshi-Uchi with a Left-Omote-Ken. Pull the right fist to the right waist.

南
South

（⑰〜⑱への動作）
Movement from ⑰ to ⑱.

（西から見る）
Seen from the west.

⑱
左足前レの字立ち。
Renojidachi
(the left foot in front)

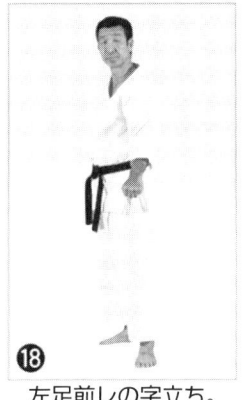

⑱-A

右足そのまま。左足を右足に少し引き寄せる。

Maintain the right foot position. Pull the left foot slightly towards the right foot.

［備考］表拳の使い方を正確に（㉒挙動も同じく）。

Make sure you use the Omote-Ken correctly. (Same as in Movement ㉒.)

掴まれた左拳を右肩前に引き寄せ、振りおろし気味に拳の第二関節で打ちつける。

① ② ③ ④

Pull the left fist (grabbed by the opponent) towards the front of the right shoulder. Throw down the left fist (second joint) and hit the opponent.

61

カンクウショウ

	15 挙 動 Move	16 挙 動 Move
手の動作 Hands	右掌中段掴み受け。左掌右手首上添え手。両拳開掌、左肘の下から右掌を円を描き、左掌は右手首を上から添えて右掌中段掴み受け。左掌右手首上添え手。 Execute a Chudan-Tsukami-Uke with the right palm. Place the left palm on the right wrist. Open both hands. Move the right palm from beneath the left elbow, drawing a circle. Place the right wrist on the left palm.	両手引き寄せ、左手を添えたまま右手を握り、右肘を右脇へ強く引きつける（甲上向）。 Pull both hands and grasp the right hand (the left hand should be touching the right hand). Firmly pull the right elbow to the right side of the body. (The back of the hand faces up.)
着眼点 Point to see	南 South （⑱〜⑲への動作） Movement from ⑱ to ⑲. ⑲ （西から見る） Seen from the west. ⑲−A	南 South ⑳
立ち方 Stance	左前屈立ち（逆半身）。 Left-Zenkutsudachi (Gyaku-Hanmi)	左脚立ち。 Stand on the left foot.
足の動作 Feet	右脚を軸として左足を南へすり出し、腰を左に回転し左膝を屈す。 Pivoting on the right foot, slide the left foot towards the south. Rotate the waist to the left and bend the left knee.	左足そのまま、右中段前蹴り（上足底）。 Maintain the left foot position. Execute a Right-Chudan-Mae-Keri (Josokutei).
留意点 Point	［備考］ややゆっくり力を込めて、両肘と両脇を強く締める。左掌は拇指を離さないで四指共に付けて添え手とする。 [Note] Slowly exert force. Pull both elbows tightly to the sides. Place the left palm on the right hand while keeping the fingers together.	
動作の分解 Kumite in detail		

方位: 北 North / 西 West / 東 East / 南 South

17 挙 動　Move

右裏拳上段縦回し打ち。
左拳は左腰に引く。

Execute a Right-Uraken-Jyodan-Tate-Mawashi-Uchi. Pull the left fist to the left waist.

南
South

（西から見る）
Seen from the west.

（⑳～㉑への動作）
Movement from ⑳ to ㉑.

（西から見る）
Seen from the west.

⑳－A

㉑

右足前交差立ち。
Right-Front-Kosadachi

㉑－A

⑯⑰挙動は敏速に行う。

Execute the Movement ⑯ and ⑰ quickly.

右足を南へ一歩飛び込み、左足を右踵の後ろに引きつける。

Jump up and place the right foot one step towards the south, pulling the left foot behind the right ankle.

交差立ちは右足に左足を充分に引きつける。右拳は左掌の後を追うように胸前から、顔の前に半円を描く。

In the Kosadachi position, pull the left foot close towards the right foot. As the right fist follows the left palm, move the right fist drawing a semi-circle from the front of the chest to the front of the face.

カンクウショウ

	18 挙 動 Move	**19 挙 動 Move**
手の動作 Hands	右中段外受け。左拳は左腰に引く。 Execute a Right-Chudan-Soto-Uke. Pull the left fist to the left waist.	左中段逆突き。右拳は右腰に引く。 Execute a Left-Chudan-Gyaku-Tsuki. Pull the right fist to the right waist.
着眼点 Point to see	南 South　（西から見る）Seen from the west.	南 South　（西から見る）Seen from the west.
立ち方 Stance	右前屈立ち（半身）。 Right-Zenkutsudachi (Hanmi)	右前屈立ち。 Right-Zenkutsudachi
足の動作 Feet	右足の位置はそのまま、左足を北へ引く。右前屈立ち。 Maintain the right foot at the same position. Pull the left foot back toward the north. Right-Zenkutsudachi.	立ち方はそのまま。 Maintain the same standing position.
留意点 Point	［備考］右拳を左脇下から肘を曲げ前腕を立てて右方へ払う。 [Note] Bend the right arm and bring the fist under the left arm. From this position, raise the upper arm and push the right fist off to the right.	

北 North / 西 West — 東 East / 南 South

⑳ 挙　動　Move	㉑ 挙　動　Move
右中段順突き。左拳は左腰に引く。	右中段外受け。左下段受け。右拳を左腰前に（甲上向）左拳を右肩前に（甲外向）。右拳は左腰前より右肩の前へ（甲右向）、肘を直角に曲げる。左拳は右肩前より脇腹の前。両拳同時に動かす。
Execute a Right-Chudan-Jun-Tsuki. Pull the left fist to the left waist.	Execute a Right Chudan-Soto-Uke and then a Left-Gedan-Uke. Hold the right fist in front of the left waist (the back of the hand facing up). Hold the left fist in front of the right shoulder (the back of the hand facing out). Move the right hand (fist) to the front of the right shoulder from the front of the left waist (the back of the hand facing to the right). Bend the elbow vertically. Move the left fist to the front of the flank from the the front of right shoulder. Move both fists at the same time.

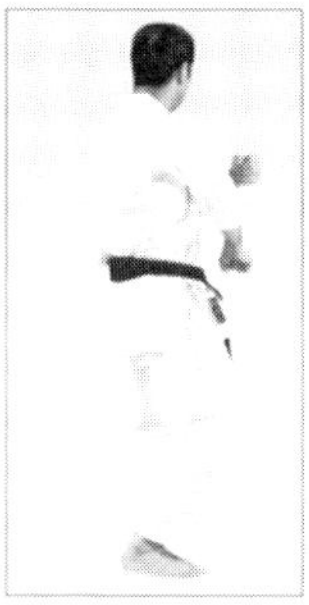

南　　　　　　　　　　　　　　　　　　　北
South　　　　　　　　　　　　　　　　　North

（西から見る）　（㉔〜㉕への動作）　　　　　　　　　　（西から見る）
Seen from the west.　Movement from ㉔ to ㉕.　　　　　Seen from the west.

㉔　　　　　　　　　　　　　　　　　　　㉕
右前屈立ち。　　　㉔-A　　　　右後屈立ち。　　　㉕-A
Right-Zenkutsudachi　　　　　Right-Kokutsudachi

立ち方はそのまま。	右脚を軸とし腰を左へ回転し、左足を北へ進める。
Maintain the same standing position.	Pivoting on the right foot, rotate the waist to the left. Move the left foot to the north.

［備考］挙動⑲・⑳は敏速に続けて連突き。	［備考］右脚を軸として外受け。下段受けを同時に行う。
[Note] In Movements ⑲ and ⑳, execute a Tsuki quickly and continuously.	[Note] Pivoting on the right foot, execute a Soto-Uke and Gedan-Uke simultaneously.

カンクウショウ

	22 挙 動 Move
手の動作 Hands	左表拳振りおろし打ち。 右拳は右腰に引く。 Execute a Furi-Oroshi-Uchi with the left fist (Omote-Ken). Pull the right fist to the right waist.
着眼点 Point to see	北 North （㉕～㉖への動作） ㉖ （西から見る） （㉖～㉗への動作） Movement from ㉕ to ㉖. Seen from the west. Movement from ㉖ to ㉗. ㉖-A
立ち方 Stance	左足前レの字立ち。 Renojidachi (the left foot in front)
北 North 西 West ― 東 East 南 South	
足の動作 Feet	右足そのまま、左足を右足に少し引き寄せる。 Maintain the right foot position. Slightly pull the left foot next to the right foot.
留意点 Point	［備考］表拳の使い方を正確に。 [Note] Make sure you use the Omote-Ken correctly.

66

23 挙　動　Move

右拳右側面上段受け。左拳左側面下段受け。両拳開掌、両腕をいったん胸前で交差し、互いに引っ張り合う。

Execute a Jodan-Uke with the right side of the right fist.
Execute a Gedan-Uke with the left side of the left fist. Open both fists.
Cross both arms in front of the chest and then strain them each other.

西
West

（西から見る）
Seen from the west.

（㉗〜㉘への動作）
Movement from ㉗ to ㉘.

㉗

右後屈立ち。
Right-Kokutsudachi

㉗-A

右足そのまま、左足を西に進める。

Maintain the right foot position. Move the left foot towards the west.

67

カンクウショウ

	24 挙 動 Move	**25** 挙 動 Move
手の動作 Hands	左側面中段諸手突き。両拳をいったん右胸前に引き寄せて両拳同時に平行に肩よりやや低めに真っ直ぐに突き伸ばす（両拳甲上向）。 Execute a Chudan-Morote-Tsuki on the left side. Pull both fists to the front of the right chest and simultaneously push out both fists in parallel, lightly lower than shoulder level straight. (The backs of both fists face up.)	左拳左側面上段受け。右拳右側面下段受け。両拳開掌、両腕をいったん胸前で交差し、互いに引っ張り合う。 Execute a Jodan-Uke with the left side of the left fist. Execute a Gedan-Uke with the right side of the right fist. Open both fists. Cross both arms in front of the chest and then strain them each other.
着眼点 Point to see	西 West	東 East
立ち方 Stance	騎馬立ち。 Kibadachi. ㉘－A (西から見る) Seen from the west. (㉘～㉙への動作) Movement from ㉘ to ㉙	左後屈立ち。 Left-Kokutsudachi (㉙～㉚への動作) Movement from ㉙ to ㉚
足の動作 Feet	西へ寄足しながら、右足を引きつける。 Make a Yoriashi towards the west and pull the right foot.	左脚を軸として、東に振り向く。 Pivoting on the left foot, turn around towards the east.
留意点 Point	両腕とも肘を伸ばして突く。（胸前並行）。 Push both arms by extending the elbows. (The arms are parallel in front of the chest.)	
動作の分解 Kumite in detail	両拳は、いったん開手し右拳は左下から抜け上げるように握りながら肘を曲げて左上段受け、同時に左拳を右肩前から左下段受け。気味に左方へ移動し、両拳を右脇下に引き寄せ、左拳、右拳を左右胸前に突き出す。鉤突きでは胸前並行に突くが、右拳は胸前並行に突くことに注意。 Open both fists. Move the right hand (making a fist again) from the lower left side upward, bend the elbow and execute a Right-Jodan-Uke. At the same time, move the left fist from the front of the right shoulder and execute a Left-Gedan-Uke. Then immediately move to the left with a Yoriashi, pull both fists to the right side of the chest, and push the left and right fists to the left side. Push both fists so they are parallel at the front of the chest. Make sure the right fist should not be in a Kagi-Tsuki form.	

68

26 挙 動　Move	27 挙 動　Move
右側面中段諸手突き。両拳をいったん左胸前に引き寄せて両拳同時に平行に肩よりやや低めに真っ直ぐに突き伸ばす（両拳甲上向）。	両掌上段棒受け。両拳開掌、左掌を上に向け、額前上へ（甲斜下向）。肘を伸ばし気味に右掌も上に向けて右脇腹前へ（甲下向）。
Execute a Chudan-Morote-Tsuki on the right side. Pull both fists in front of the left chest, and simultaneously push both fists out straight in parallel, slightly lower than shoulder level. (The backs of both fists face up.)	Execute a Jodan-Bo-Uke with both palms. Open both fists. Turn the left palm upward and hold it in front of the forehead (the back of the hand is facing slantingly down). Lightly extending the right elbow, hold the right palm facing upward in front of the right flank.

東
East

（㉚〜㉛への動作）
Movement from ㉚ to ㉛.

北
North

（西から見る）
Seen from the west.

㉚　騎馬立ち。
Kibadachi

㉛　左後屈立ち。
Left-Kokutsudachi

㉛-A

東へ寄足しながら、左足を引きつける。	左足を半歩引き寄せ、その左脚を軸として右足を北へ一歩前方へすり出す。
Make a Yoriashi towards the east and pull the left foot.	Pull the left foot a half-step. Pivoting on the left foot, slide the right foot one step towards the north.
両腕とも肘を伸ばして突く（胸前並行）。	27・28・29挙動の棒受け・棒押し込みからの飛びは着地とタイミングを大切に。
Push both arms by extending the elbows. (The arms are parallel in front of the chest.)	The timing of the jump from the Bo-Uke/Bo-Oshikomi position in Movements 27, 28 and 29 and the landing is critical.

カンクウショウ

28 挙 動 Move

手の動作 Hands

棒押し込み。受けた棒を掴み、両手を捻って相手の後方へ押し込むように両手を握り締め、左拳（甲下向）を右乳下に、右拳（甲上向）を斜め下へ、右肘を伸ばす。

Execute a Bo-Oshikomi. Grab the pole (attacked), while still holding the pole, twist your hands, pushing the opponent's hands (also holding the pole) behind him. Move the left fist (the back of the hand facing down) to the lower part of the right chest. Move the right fist (the back of the hand facing up) to the lower side. Extend the right elbow.

着眼点 Point to see

北 North

（㉛～㉜への動作） Movement from ㉛ to ㉜.

（西から見る） Seen from the west.

（㉜～㉝への動作） Movement from ㉜ to ㉝.

㉜

㉜－A

立ち方 Stance

右足前不動立ち。 Right-Front-Fudodachi

北 North / 西 West / 東 East / 南 South

足の動作 Feet

北へ寄足。 Yoriashi towards north.

両脚を同時に高くかい込み、（あぐらをかくように）左回りにその場で高く飛び上がり一回転し両足元の位置。

Move both feet at the same time and jump high (similar to sittig crossed-legged), turning to the left at that location, making a complete spin, both feet land in the original positions.

留意点 Point

動作の分解 Kumite in detail

両掌上段受けし、棒を掴み、両掌を捻りながら斜め下に激しく押し込み相手の体勢を崩す。

① ②
Execute a Jodan-Uke with both palms. Grab the pole and twist both palms down, then push hard to brake the opponent's posture.

更に反撃する相手が脛を払うのを、両足をかい込み高く飛び上がり一回転する。40センチ〜50センチ以上の高さに飛び上がること。

① ②
When the opponent hits your shins, jump high bending both legs and rotate once. Jump at least 40-50 centimeters.

	29 挙 動 Move	**30** 挙 動 Move	**31** 挙 動 Move
	右手刀中段受け。 Execute a Chudan-Uke with the Right-Shuto.	両拳右腰構え。左拳（甲前向）を右拳（甲下向）の上に重ねる。 Hold both fists on the right waist. Place the left fist (the back of the hand facing front) on the right fist (the back of the hand facing down).	左裏拳上段横回し打ち。右拳はそのまま。 Execute a Jodan-Yoko-Mawashi-Uchi with a left Uraken. The right fist remains in the same position.
(㉜～㉝への動作) Movement from ㉜ to ㉝. 	北 North  ㉝	 西 West ㉞	 西 West ㉟
	 左後屈立ち。 Left-Kokutsudachi.	 右脚立ち。 Stand on the right foot.	右脚立ち。 Stand on the right foot.
		右脚を軸に左足裏を右膝横に添え、横蹴り上げの構え。右膝横に軽く付ける。 Pivoting on the right foot, place the bottom of the left foot on the side of the right knee and stand in a Yoko-Keriage.	西へ左中段横蹴り上げ。 Execute a Left-Chudan-Yoko-Keriage towards the west.

［備考］両足元の位置に接地と同時に右手刀中段受けをする。

[Note] When both feet land in the original position, execute a Chudan-Uke with a Right-Shuto.

③

71

カンクウショウ

		32 挙　動　Move
手の動作 Hands		右前猿臂。右肘を左掌に当てる。 Execute an Empi with the right elbow (hit the right elbow against the left palm).
着眼点 Point to see	（㉟～㊱への動作） Movement from ㉟ to ㊱. 引き足をとるところ。 Executing a Hiki-Ashi	西 West ㊱ 左前屈立ち。 Left-Zenkutsudachi　㊱-A （西から見る） Seen from the west.
立ち方 Stance		
北 North 西 West ― 東 East 南 South		
足の動作 Feet		左足を西へおろし腰を左転。 Lower the left foot towards the west and turn the waist to the left.
留意点 Point		[備考] 挙動㉚・㉛・㉜は続けて早く。 [Note] Do Movements ㉚,㉛, and ㉜ quickly and continuously.

72

33 挙 動 Move	34 挙 動 Move
両拳左腰構え。右拳（甲前向）を左拳（甲下向）の上に重ねる。 Hold both fists on the left waist. Place the right fist (the back of the hand facing front) on the left fist (the back of the hand facing down).	右裏拳上段横回し打ち。左拳はそのまま。 Execute a Jodan-Yoko-Mawashi-Uchi with a Right-Uraken. The left fist remains in the same position.

東
East

（西から見る）
Seen from the west.

東
East

(㊲〜㊴への動作)
Movement from ㊳ to ㊴.

㊲ 左脚立ち。
Stand on the left foot.

㊲-A

㊳ 左脚立ち。
Stand on the left foot.

左脚を軸に右足裏を左膝横に添え横蹴上げの構え。

Pivoting on the left foot, place the bottom of the right foot on the side of the left knee and stand in a Yoko-Keriage.

東へ右中段横蹴上げ。

Execute a Right-Chudan-Yoko-Keriage towards the east.

カンクウショウ

	35 挙 動 Move	36 挙 動 Move
手の動作 Hands	左前猿臂。左肘を右掌に当てる。 Execute an Empi with the left elbow (hit the left elbow against the right palm).	右掌中段掴み受け。左掌右手首上添え手。両拳開掌、左肘の下から右掌を円を描き、左掌は右手首を上から添えて右掌中段掴み受け。左掌右手首上添え手。 Execute a Right-Chudan-Tsukami-Uke. Place the left palm on the right wrist. Open both palms. Move the right palm from under the left elbow by drawing a circle. Place the right wrist on the left palm from above.
着眼点 Point to see	東 East　　　　　（西から見る） 　　　　　　　　Seen from the west.	北 North　　　　　（西から見る） 　　　　　　　　Seen from the west.
立ち方 Stance	39　　　　　39-A 右前屈立ち。 Right-Zenkutsudachi	40　　　　　40-A 左膝屈。 Left-Hizakutsu
足の動作 Feet	右足を東へおろし腰を右転。 Lower the right foot towards the east and turn the waist to the right.	両足の位置はそのまま、右脚を軸として腰を左に回転し、左膝を屈し右膝伸ばし両足を左転する。 Maintain both feet in the same position. Pivoting on the right foot, turn the waist to the left. Bend the left knee and stretch the right knee.
留意点 Point	[備考] 挙動33・34・35は続けて早く。 [Note] Do Movements 33, 34, and 35 quickly and continuously.	[備考] ややゆっくり力を込めて、両肘と両脇を強く締める。左掌は拇指を離さないで四指共に付けて添え手とする。 [Note] Slowly exert force. Pull both elbows tightly to the sides. Place the left palm on the right hand while keeping the fingers together.

37 挙　動　Move

両手引き寄せ、左手を添えたまま右手を握り、右肘を右脇へ強く引きつける（甲上向）。

Pull both hands. Placing the left hand on the right wrist, close the right hand. Pull the right elbow next to the right side tightly. (The back of the hand faces up.)

38 挙　動　Move

右裏拳上段縦回し打ち。左拳は左腰に引く。

Execute a Right-Uraken-Jyodan-Tate-Mawashi-Uchi. Pull the left fist to the left waist.

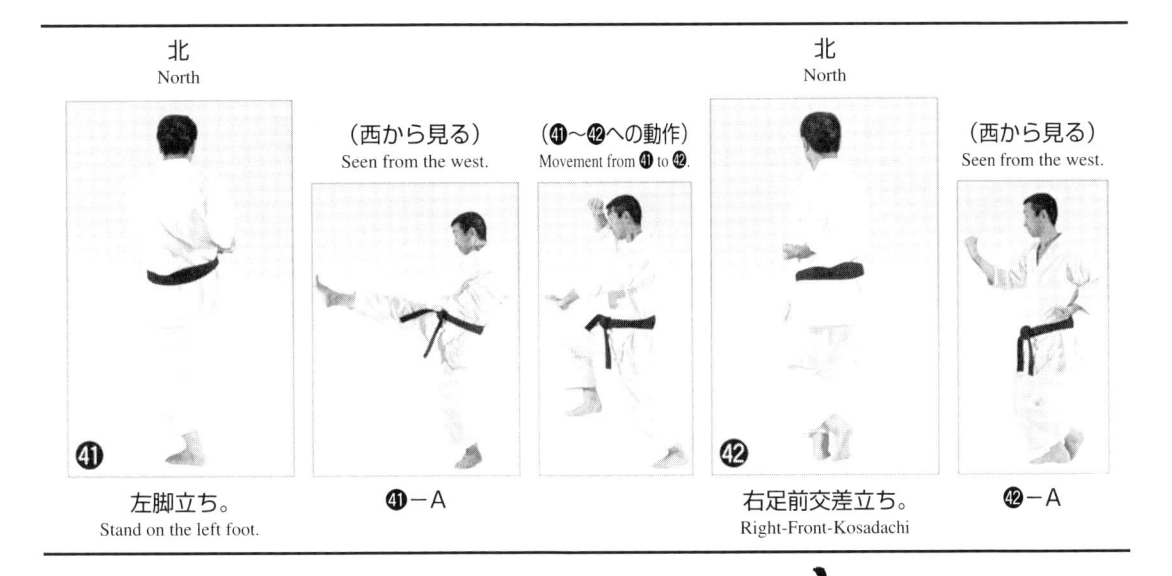

北
North

（西から見る）
Seen from the west.

（㊶～㊷への動作）
Movement from ㊶ to ㊷.

㊶
左脚立ち。
Stand on the left foot.

㊶-A

北
North

（西から見る）
Seen from the west.

㊷
右足前交差立ち。
Right-Front-Kosadachi

㊷-A

左足そのまま、右中段前蹴り（上足底）。

Maintain the left foot position. Execute a Right-Chudan-Mae-Keri (Josokutei).

右足を北へ一歩飛び込み、左足を右踵の後ろに引きつける。

Jump up and place the right foot one step forward the north, pulling the left foot behind the right ankle.

交差立ちは右足に左足を充分に引きつける。右拳は左掌の後を追うように胸前から、顔の前に半円を描く。

In the Kosadachi position, pull the left foot close towards the right foot. As the right fist follows the left fist, move the right fist drawing a semi-circle from the front of the chest to the front of the face.

カンクウショウ

39 挙動 Move

手の動作 / Hands

右中段外受け。左拳は左腰に引く。

Execute a Right-Chudan-Soto-Uke. Pull the left fist to the left waist.

着眼点 / Point to see

北 / North

（㊷〜㊸への動作）
Movement from ㊷ to ㊸.

㊸

右前屈立ち（半身）。
Right-Zenkutsudachi (Hanmi)

立ち方 / Stance

北 North / 西 West / 東 East / 南 South

足の動作 / Feet

右足の位置はそのまま、左足を南へ引く。右前屈立ち。

Maintain the right foot position. Pull the left foot toward the south. Right-Zenkutsudachi.

留意点 / Point

[備考] 右拳を左脇下から肘を曲げ前腕を立てて右方へ払う。

[Note] Bend the right elbow from the left side of the arm and raise the right forearm and push the right fist off to the right.

40 挙 動　Move

左中段逆突き。右拳は右腰に引く。

Execute a Left-Chudan-Gyaku-Tsuki. Pull the right fist to the right waist.

北
North

(西から見る)
Seen from the west.

㊹

右前屈立ち。
Right-Zenkutsudachi

㊹－A

立ち方はそのまま。

Maintain the same standing position.

41 挙 動　Move

右中段順突き。左拳は左腰に引く。

Execute a Right-Chudan-Jun-Tsuki. Pull the left fist to the left waist.

北
North

(西から見る)
Seen from the west.

㊺

右前屈立ち。
Right-Zenkutsudachi

㊺－A

立ち方はそのまま。

Maintain the same standing position.

[備考] 挙動㊵・㊶は敏速に続けて連突き。

[Note] In Movements ㊵ and ㊶, execute a Tsuki quickly and continuously.

カンクウショウ

手の動作 / Hands

左拳開掌、左手首後方中段掛け受け。
両掌肘立て伏せ。

Open the left fist. Execute a Koho-Chudan-Kake-Uke with the left wrist. Open both hands and support the body with a Hijitate-Fuse.

着眼点 / Point to see

（㊺〜㊻への動作）
Movement from ㊺ to ㊻.

立ち方 / Stance

北 North / 西 West / 東 East / 南 South

足の動作 / Feet

立ち方そのまま、腰を左に回転し後方正面に振り向きながら左脚を軸として、腰を左に回転しながら右足を三日月形に高く回して足底を左掌に当てて、右中段三日月蹴り。

Maintain the same standing position. Turn the waist to the left and turn facing back. Pivoting on the left foot, rotate the waist to the left and at the same time kick the right foot as if drawing a crescent. Touch the bottom of the right foot against the left palm and execute a Right-Chudan-Mikazuki-Keri.

留意点 / Point

［備考］左前腕を下（甲上向）、右前腕を上に（甲上向）左手を右肘の下から後方中段へ横に円を描いて伸ばす（甲後向）、右拳右腰に引く（甲下向）。

Hold the left forearm down (the back of the hand facing up) and hold the right forearm up (the back of the hand facing up). Extend the left hand from beneath the right elbow to a back-Chudan, drawing a circle horizontally (the back of the hand facing back). Pull the right fist to the right waist (the back of the hand facing down).

動作の分解 / Kumite in detail

右前屈立ちのまま、振り向きながら、腰を左に回転させ左掌をゆっくりと左肩の高さに伸ばし、左脚を軸に右足中段三日月蹴りを行う。相手の中段突きに払い、左後段三日月蹴り飛ばし相手の中段突きに払い、左後ろ蹴りを行う。軸足はステップしないことに注意。

While standing in a Right-Zenkutsudachi, rotate the waist to the left and turn back. While turning back, slowly extend and raise the left palm to left shoulder height. Pivoting on the left foot, execute a Right-Chudan-Mikazuki-Keri by kicking the right foot to shake off the opponent's Chudan-Tuski, then execute a Left-Ushiro-Keri. Do not step the left foot.

42 挙　動　Move

両掌肘立て伏せ。

Open both hands and support the body with a Hijitate-Fuse.

北
North

（㊺～㊻への動作）
Movement from ㊺ to ㊻.

㊻

右足前伏せ（右前屈）。
Execute a Mae-Fuse with the right foot.
(Right-Zenkutsu)

（西から見る）
Seen from the west.

㊻－A

左足の踵を臀部に付けるようにかい込んで飛び、一回転。

Bend the left leg backwards, as if touching the heel to the hip and jump and make a complete spin.

三日月蹴りは膝を高く、かい込む（高く飛び上がって蹴らないこと）。

Execute a Mikazuki-Keri by raising the knee high. (Do not kick at the highest point during the jump.)

カンクウショウ

	43 挙　動　Move	**44** 挙　動　Move
手の動作 Hands	左手刀下段受け。右手刀胸前構え（低め）。 Execute a Gedan-Uke with a Left-Shuto. Hold a Right-Shuto in front of the chest (in the low position).	右手刀中段受け。左手刀胸前。 Execute a Chudan-Uke with a Right-Shuto. Hold the Left-Shuto in front of the chest.
着眼点 Point to see	北 North　　㊸　　㊼－A （西から見る）Seen from the west.　（㊼〜㊽への動作）Movement from ㊼ to ㊽.	北 North　　㊽　　㊽－A （西から見る）Seen from the west.
立ち方 Stance	右後屈立ち。 Right-Kokutsudachi	左後屈立ち。 Left-Kokutsudachi
足の動作 Feet	両足同時に、その場で左右踏み替えて低い右後屈立ち。 Switch the positions of both feet simultaneously and stand in a low Right-Kokutsudachi.	右足を北にすり出す。 Slide the right foot towards the north.
留意点 Point		

80

45 挙動 Move	**46** 挙動 Move
左中段外受け。右拳右腰に引く。 Execute a Left-Chudan-Soto-Uke. Pull the right fist to the right waist.	右中段順突き。左拳左腰に引く。 Execute a Right-Chudan-Jun-Tsuki. Pull the left fist to the left waist.
東 East	東 East
(48〜49への動作) Movement from 48 to 49. 49 左前屈立ち（半身）。 Left-Zenkutsudachi (Hanmi)	50 右前屈立ち。 Right-Zenkutsudachi	(50〜51への動作) Movement from 50 to 51.
右脚を軸として体を左に回転させて、左足を東に移動させる。 Pivoting on the right foot, rotate the body to the left and move the left foot towards the east.	左脚を軸として、右足を東へすり出す。 Pivoting on the left foot, slide the right foot towards the east.

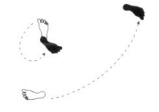

カンクウショウ

	47 挙動 Move	48 挙 動 Move		
手の動作 Hands	右中段外受け。左拳左腰に引く。 Execute a Right-Chudan-Soto-Uke. Pull the left fist to the left waist.	左中段順突き。右拳右腰に引く。 Execute a Left-Chudan-Jun-Tsuki. Pull the right fist to the right waist.		
着眼点 Point to see	西 West	西 West	（西から見る） Seen from the west.	(52〜53への動作) Movement from 52 to 53.
立ち方 Stance	右前屈立ち（半身）。 Right-Zenkutsudachi (Hanmi)	左前屈立ち。 Left-Zenkutsudachi	52−A	
足の動作 Feet	左脚を軸とし体を右に回転させて、右足を西に移動させる。 Pivoting on the left foot, rotate the body to the right and move the right foot towards the west.	右脚を軸として左足を西へすり出す。 Pivoting on the right foot, slide the left foot towards the west.		
留意点 Point		気合。 Kiai.		

北 North / 西 West / 東 East / 南 South

止め Stop	直立 Stand
	両手は開いて大腿部両側に付けて伸ばす。 Open both hands and stretch the arms down to the sides of the thighs.

南
South

南
South

㊳
八字立ち。
Hachijidachi

㊴
結び立ち。
Musubidachi

八字立ち。
Hachijidachi

結び立ち。
Musubidachi

右足の位置はそのまま、左足を戻しながら用意の姿勢にかえる。

Maintain the right foot position, Pull back the left foot to the original position, return to the Ready position.

83

燕飛
エンピ

[特　徴]

　身体の伸縮の多い形。いきなり身を沈めて突きと蹴りを受け、飛び込み反転しての敏速果敢な攻防の連続から最後は上段突きを左掌で受けると同時に、右手を相手の股間に差し入れて一回転しての肩車投げで終わる。さながら飛び舞う燕のような技の動きから、松濤館流では「燕飛」と命名した。別名を、伝えた武人の名といわれる「ワンシュウ」という。

ENPI

[Characteristics]

This Kata has a lot of body stretchings and contractions. The player quickly lowers the body, receives the Tsuki and Keri, and then plunges and turns toward the opponent. Executing a series of quick and bold offensive and defensive actions, at the end the player blocks the Jodan-Tsuki with the left palm and at the same time, inserts the right hand into the opponent's crotch, rotating once, and ends with the Kataguruma-Nage. Because the movements in this waza represent a flying swallow, Shotokan-Ryu named this Kata as "Enpi". Another name is Wanshu, which is said to be the name of the warrior who conceived the nameterm.

エンピ

	直立 Stand	用意 Ready	1 挙動 Move	2 挙動 Move
手の動作 Hands	両手は開いて大腿部両側に付けて伸ばす。 Open both hands and stretch the arms down to the sides of the thighs.	左掌右拳左腰、左掌（甲左向）を左腰に、右拳（甲前向）を左掌に当てる。 Left palm, right fist, left waist. Place the left palm (the back of the hand facing left) on the left waist. Place the right fist (the back of the hand facing forward) on the left palm.	右拳下段受け（甲前向）、左拳（甲下向）水月前に構える。 Execute a Gedan-Uke with the right fist (the back of the hand facing forward). Keep the left fist (the back of the hand facing down) in front of the abdomen.	両拳左腰構え。右拳（甲前向）を左拳（甲下向）の上に重ねる。 Both fists are held on the left waist. Place the right fist (the back of the hand facing forward) on the left fist (the back of the hand facing down).
着眼点 Point to see	南 South	南 South	西南 Westsouth	西南 Westsouth
立ち方 Stance	結び立ち。 Musubidachi	閉足立ち。 Heisokudachi	右脚折敷・左脚立て。 The right leg is in a kneeling position and the left leg is bent.	八字立ち(歩幅やや広め)。 Hachijidachi (a little space between the legs)
足の動作 Feet	結び立ち。 Musubidachi	閉足立ち。 Heisokudachi (白から黒へ動く。) (Move from White to Black.)	顔を右に向ける。右膝は、左足踵の線上（右膝と左足踵の間、拳1つ）。 Turn the face to the right. The right knee should be aligned with the left ankle on the one line (space one fist between the right knee and the left ankle).	その場に立ち上がり、歩幅やや広めの八字立ちとなる。 Stand up at that position in a Hachijidachi while the legs are a rather widely apart.
留意点 Point			足幅が広くなりすぎないよう。 Do not space the legs too far apart.	
動作の分解 Kumite in detail				右側からの蹴りを捌いて受け払う。腰の鋭い回転がポイントである。左足の横への開き、右膝の折り敷き、右腕の払いは同時でなければいけない。 Fend off the kick (Keri) from the right side, and push the leg out (Uke-Harai) using the right forearm. It is very important to twist the waist quickly. Moving the left leg to the side, bending the right knee and fending off with the right arm must all be done simultaneously.

方位: 北 North / 西 West / 東 East / 南 South

3 挙動 Move	4 挙動 Move	5 挙動 Move
右下段払い。左拳はそのまま、右拳を右膝上の位置へ（甲上向）左拳左腰に引く。 Right-Gedan-Harai. Keep the left fist as is. Move the right fist above the right knee (the back of the hand facing up). Pull the left fist to the left waist.	左腕水流れの構え。肘から先を直角に曲げ水月の前へ（甲上向）。右拳右腰に引く。 The left arm is in the Mizu-Nagare position. Bend the elbow vertically to a right angle and hold it in front of the abdomen. Pull the right fist (the back of the hand facing up) to the right waist.	左下段払い（甲上向）。右拳右腰に引く。 Execute a Left-Gedan-Harai (the back of the hand facing up). Pull the right fist to the right waist.
西 West	南 South	南 South
	（❻～❼への動作） Movement from ❻ to ❼.		（西から見る） Seen from the west.
❺	❻	❼	❼-A
右脚前屈（半身）。 Right leg-Zenkutsu (Hanmi)	騎馬立ち。 Kibadachi	左前屈立ち（半身）。 Left-Zenkutsudachi (Hanmi)	
右脚前屈。 Right leg - Zenkutsu	両足の位置は、そのまま。正面に向き騎馬立ちになる。 Both feet remain in the same position. Face forward and stand in a Kibadachi position.	右脚を軸として前方正面へ左足をすり出す。 Pivoting on the right foot, slide the left leg to the front.	
[備考] 右拳を左肩前より反動をつけて下段払い。 [Note] Execute a Gedan-Harai with the recoiling right fist from the front side of the left shoulder.	水流れの構えは、左拳先が少し下がり気味。 In the Mizu-Nagare position, the forward end of the left fist is facing slightly downward.		

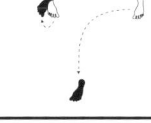

エンピ

6 挙動 Move

手の動作 Hands

右上段揚げ突き。相手の左上段突きを下から上にはね上げ、相手の顎を突き上げる（甲上向）。左拳左腰に引く。

Execute a Right-Jodan-Age-Tsuki. Fend off the Left-Jodan-Tsuki (from the opponent) by pushing the arm up from the lower side, and push the opponent's jaw up. (The back of the right hand is facing up.) Pull the left fist to the left waist.

着眼点 Point to see

南
South

（西から見る）
Seen from the west.

（❽〜❾への動作）
Movement from ❽ to ❾.

立ち方 Stance

左前屈立ち（逆半身）。
Left-Zenkutsudachi (Gyaku-Hanmi)

❽-A

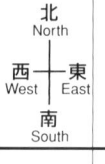

北 North
西 West — 東 East
南 South

足の動作 Feet

立ち方はそのまま。
Maintain the same standing position.

留意点 Point

[備考] 上体をやや左に捻る。
[Note] Twist the upper body slightly to the left.

[備考] 上段揚げ突きの後、すかさず敏速に飛び込む。
[Note] After the Jodan-Age-Tsuki, leap quickly.

手の開きと、膝胸前かい込みを同時に行い、左足を右踵の後ろに交差する。
Simultaneously opening the palm and moving the right knee towards the chest, cross the left leg behind the right ankle.

動作の分解 Kumite in detail

右拳揚げ突きで顎を攻撃、すかさず開手して胸倉または頭髪を掴み引きながら、右足を高くかい込み飛び込み左下段突き。左足を右足踵の後ろにしっかりと引きつけ正確堅固な交差立ちとなる。身を十分屈するが、へっぴり腰にならないように注意すること。

① ② ③

Execute a Uken-Age-Tsuki to hit the opponent's jaw. Immediately open the fist, grab the opponent's collar or hair, jump high by bending the right foot, plunge into the opponent, and then execute a Left-Gedan-Tsuki. Pull the left foot so it is behind the right ankle, then precisely and firmly stand in a Kosadachi. In this move, you bend your body low but make sure to hold your body self-confidently.

7 挙　動　Move	**8** 挙　動　Move
右拳開掌・右拳左肩前上。左拳下段突き。	右下段払い。左拳は左腰に引く。
Open the right fist. Place the right fist on the left shoulder. Execute a Gedan-Tsuki with the left fist.	Execute a Right-Gedan-Harai. Pull the left fist to the left waist.

南　　　　　　　　　　　　　　南
South　　　　　　　　　　　　South

（❾〜❿への動作）
Movement from ❾ to ❿.

（西から見る）
Seen from the west.

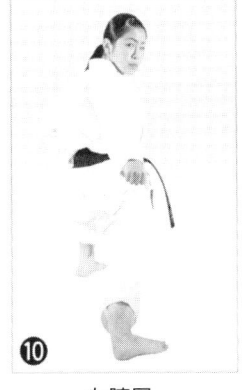

❾　　　　　　　　　　　　　　❿　　　　　　　❿－A

右足前交差立ち。　　　　　　　左膝屈。
Kosadachi (right foot in front)　The left knee is bent.

右膝を胸前にかい込み、右足で前方正面へ飛び込み右脚を屈して体重を支え、左足を右踵の後ろに交差する。	右足の位置はそのまま、左足を一歩後ろへ引き、やや広めに左膝を屈し右膝を伸ばす。
Move the right knee towards the chest. Jump forward with the right foot; bend the right leg forward to support the weight. Move the left leg behind the right ankle so that the legs are crossed.	The right foot remains in the same position. Pull the left foot one step. Bend the left knee rather widely and stretch the right knee.

	左足を右踵の後ろに交差する。	**7**挙動で突いた左拳を相手に掴まれたので、相手の手首を打って引き抜く気持ち。
	Stand with both legs crossed with the right leg in front.	In Movement **7**, the opponent grabbed the left fist you pushed. It appears to make this a hitting movement (hitting the opponent's wrist) and pull out your left fist.

挙動**7**で突いた左下段突きを相手にとられた想定で、右拳を左肩前から捻りながら下段払いまたは拳槌で打ち払う。交差立ちから鋭い腰の回転から左膝立ちになり、右拳を左肩前から捻りながら下段払いのように、拳槌で打ち払う。

① ② ③

Assume that you have executed a Left-Gedan-Tsuki in Movement **7** and the opponent has grabbed you. Turn and twist your right fist from the front of the left shoulder and execute a Gedan-Harai or Kentsui to beat away the opponent. From the cross-legged position, rotate the waist sharply to be in the left-knee position. Swinging down the right fist slantingly from the front side of the left shoulder, cut the opponent's attack with Kentsui as done in Gedan-Harai.

エンピ

	9 挙 動 Move	**10** 挙 動 Move
手の動作 Hands	左下段払い。右拳右腰に引く。 Execute a Left-Gedan-Harai. Pull the right fist to the right waist.	右上段揚げ突き。相手の左上段突きを下から上にはね上げ、相手の顎を突き上げる（甲上向）。左拳左腰に引く。 Execute a Right-Jodan-Age-Tsuki. Fend off the Left-Jodan-Tsuki (from the opponent) by pushing the arm up from the lower side, and push the opponent's jaw up. (The back of the right hand is facing up.) Pull the left fist to the left waist.
着眼点 Point to see	北 North　（西から見る）Seen from the west.　⓫　⓫-A 左前屈立ち（半身）。 Left-Zenkutsudachi (Hanmi)	北 North　（西から見る）Seen from the west.　（⓬〜⓭への動作）Movement from ⓬ to ⓭.　⓬　⓬-A 左前屈立ち（逆半身）。 Left-Zenkutsudachi (Gyaku-Hanmi)
立ち方 Stance		
北 North 西 West 東 East 南 South		
足の動作 Feet	右脚を軸として左足を少し引き気味に左前屈立ち。 Pivoting on the right foot, slightly pull the left foot and stand in a Left-Zenkutsudachi.	立ち方はそのまま。 Maintain the same standing position.
留意点 Point		

11 挙 動 Move

右拳開掌・右拳左肩前
上、左拳下段突き。

Open the right fist. Place the right fist on the left shoulder. Execute a Gedan-Tsuki with the left fist.

⓭ 右足前交差立ち。
Kosadachi(right foot in front)

⓭-A

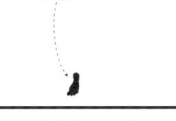

右膝を胸前にかい込み、右足を前方正面へ飛び込み右足を屈して体重を支え、左足を右踵の後ろに交差する。

Move the right knee towards the chest. Jump forward with the right foot; bend the right leg forward to support the weight. Move the left leg behind the right ankle so that the legs are crossed.

手の開きと、膝胸前かい込みを同時に行い、左足を右踵の後ろに交差する。

Simultaneously opening the palm and moving the right knee towards the chest, cross the left leg behind the right ankle.

12 挙 動 Move

右下段払い。左拳は左腰
に引く。

Execute a Right-Gedan-Harai. Pull the left fist to the left waist.

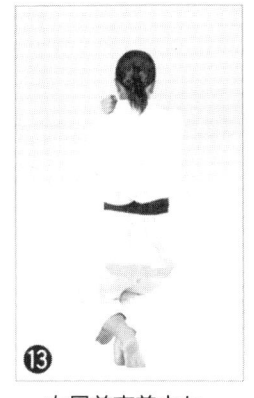

⓮ 左膝屈。
The left knee is bent.

⓮-A

右足の位置はそのまま、左足を一歩後ろへ引き、やや広めに左膝を屈し右膝を伸ばす。

Keeping the right foot in the same position, pull the left foot one step. Bend the left knee rather widely and stretch the right knee.

91

エンピ

13 挙 動　Move

手の動作 / Hands

左下段払い。右拳は右腰に引く。

Execute a Left-Gedan-Harai. Pull the right fist to the right waist.

着眼点 / Point to see

南 / South

（西から見る） / Seen from the west.

（⑮〜⑯への動作） / Movement from ⑮ to ⑯.

立ち方 / Stance

左前屈立ち(半身)。
Left-Zenkutsudachi (Hanmi)

⑮ ─ A

北 North / 西 West — 東 East / 南 South

足の動作 / Feet

右脚を軸として左足を少し引き気味に左前屈立ち。

Pivoting on the right foot, slightly pull the left foot and stand in a Left-Zenkutsudachi.

留意点 / Point

14 挙 動　Move

左手は左膝と同じく動かし右肩前から目の高さに上げ半円を描き、左掌を左斜め前上方に構える（甲左斜前向）。右拳右腰へ引く。

The left hand motion is similar to the left knee motion. Raise the hand from the front of the right shoulder to eye-level, draw a semi-circle and hold the left palm pointing front upper left. (The back of the hand faces to the front upper left.)
Pull the right fist to the right waist.

15 挙 動　Move

右手首を左掌に打ちつける（甲前向）。

Hit the right wrist on the left palm. (The back of the hand faces front.)

東南
Eastsouth

（西から見る）
Seen from the west.

⑯

騎馬立ち。
Kibadachi

⑯-A

南
South

（西から見る）　（⑰〜⑱への動作）
Seen from the west.　Movement from ⑰ to ⑱.

⑰

左脚立ち。
Stand on the left foot.

⑰-A

右足の位置と右拳はそのまま、腰を右足の上に移しながら左脚を右胸前にかい込み、左手左足ともに半円を描き、左側方におろし騎馬立ち。

Maintain the right foot position. Keep the right fist in the same position. Move the waist so that the weight of the body is on the right leg; raise the left leg in front of the right side of the chest. The left hand and left leg draw a semi-circle. Lower the left leg and stand in a Kibadachi.

左足の位置はそのままで、手の動作と同時に右足の甲を左脚裏に付ける。

The left foot remains in the same position. When the hand is moving, move the instep of the right foot to the back of the left leg.

[備考] 左肘と左膝を同じ間隔に保ちながら、大きくゆっくり回す気持ち、目は左手の動きに常に注いで、ともに回す（左肘90度に曲げる）。

[Note] Keep the same distance between the left elbow and the left knee, it appears to rotate the arm and the foot widely and slowly. Keep looking at the left hand movement. (The left elbow is bent at a 90-degree angle.)

[備考] 右拳を大きく振り回す。顔は正面を向く。

[Note] Swing the right fist widely. The face is facing front.

気合。

Kiai.

エンピ

16 挙動 Move

手の動作 / Hands

左手刀を右脇下からゆっくり半円を描いて水平に回し、左肩前方へ肘を伸ばし左縦手刀中段受け。右拳は右腰へ引く。

Turn the Left-Shuto slowly and horizontally from the lower side of the right armpit as if drawing a semi-circle. Extend the elbow so that it is horizontal to the front of the left shoulder and execute a Chudan-Uke with a Left-Tate-Shuto. Pull the right fist to the right waist.

着眼点 / Point to see

南 / South

⑱

⑱-A （西から見る） Seen from the west.

立ち方 / Stance

騎馬立ち。 Kibadachi

足の動作 / Feet

左足の位置はそのまま。

Maintain the left foot in the same position.

留意点 / Point

[備考] 右手を開いて相手の手を掴む気持ちで握り締める。左手は前方へ水平に伸ばし、相手の中段突きを内から受ける気持ち。左右両方とも、ゆっくり同時に動かす。

[Note] Open the right hand and grasp again as if you are grabbing the opponent's hand. Extend the left hand to the front horizontally, as if you are fending off (from inside) the opponent's Chudan-Tsuki. Move both arms slowly and simultaneously.

17 挙動 Move

手の動作 / Hands

相手を左手で掴んで引き寄せながら右拳中段突き。左拳左腰に引く。

Grab the opponent with the left hand. Execute a Chudan-Tsuki with the right fist while pulling the opponent. Pull the left fist to the left waist.

着眼点 / Point to see

南 / South

⑲

⑲-A （西から見る） Seen from the west.

立ち方 / Stance

騎馬立ち。 Kibadachi

足の動作 / Feet

立ち方はそのまま。

Maintain the same standing position.

18 挙動 Move

手の動作 / Hands

左拳中段突き、右拳右腰に引く。

Execute a Chudan-Tsuki with the left fist. Pull the right fist to the right waist.

着眼点 / Point to see

南 / South

⑳

立ち方 / Stance

騎馬立ち。 Kibadachi

足の動作 / Feet

立ち方はそのまま。

Maintain the same standing position.

留意点 / Point

[備考] 挙動 17・18 は敏速に続けて連突き。

[Note] Movements 17 and 18 must be quick and continuous. (Ren-Tsuki).

動作の分解 / Kumite in detail

挙動⑮で右拳を左掌に打ちつけて突っ込んでくる右脇突きに誘い、隙ができた右脇に突きを誘い込んでくる相手を引き寄せ、更に左中段突きで反撃する。右中段突きで払い、相手を掴み引き寄せ連続突き

① ②

In Movement 15, you hit the left palm with the right fist and the opponent executes a Tsuki into the blind spot on the right side of your body. Shake off the opponent's Tsuki with your left hand, pull the opponent towards you, and then execute a Right-Chudan-Tsuki and a Left-Chudan-Tsuki continuously to make the counterattack.

19 挙動 Move	20 挙 動 Move
左下段払い。右拳右腰に引く。	右上段揚げ突き。相手の左上段突きを下から上にはね上げ、相手の顎を突き上げる（甲上向）。左拳左腰に引く。
Execute a Left-Gedan-Harai. Pull the right fist to the right waist.	Execute a Right-Jodan-Age-Tsuki. Fend off the Left-Jodan-Tsuki (from the opponent) by pushing the arm up from the lower side, and push the opponent's jaw up. (The back of the right hand is facing up.) Pull the left fist to the left waist.

(⑳〜㉑への動作)
Movement from ⑳ to ㉑.

東
East

東
East

(西から見る) (㉒〜㉓への動作)
Seen from the west. Movement from ㉒ to ㉓.

㉑ 左前屈立ち（半身）。
Left-Zenkutsudachi (Hanmi)

㉒ 左前屈立ち（逆半身）。
Left-Zenkutsudachi (Gyaku-Hanmi)

㉒−A

右足の位置はそのまま。	立ち方はそのまま。
Maintain the right foot in the same position.	Maintain the same standing position.

［備考］上体をやや左に捻る。

[Note] Slightly twist the upper body to the left.

エンピ

	21 挙動 Move	**22** 挙動 Move	**23** 挙動 Move
手の動作 Hands	右手刀中段受け。左手刀胸前。 Execute a Chudan-Uke with Right-Shuto. Pull the Left-Shuto to the front of the chest.	左手刀中段受け。右手刀胸前。 Execute a Chudan-Uke with Left-Shuto. Pull the Right-Shuto to the front of the chest.	右拳中段突き・左拳左腰に引く。 Execute a Chudan-Tsuki with the right fist. Pull the left fist to the left waist.
着眼点 Point to see	東 East	東 East	東 East
立ち方 Stance	左後屈立ち。 Left-Kokutsudachi	右後屈立ち。 Right-Kokutsudachi	右後屈立ち。 Right-Kokutsudachi
足の動作 Feet	左足の位置そのまま。右足をすり出しながら後屈立ち。 Maintain the left foot in the same position. Slide the right foot toward the front and stand in a Kokutsudachi.	右足を左足の位置まで引き左足を右足のあった位置にすり出す。 Pull the right leg into the position of the left leg. Slide the left foot to the position where the right foot was.	立ち方はそのまま。 Maintain the same standing position.
留意点 Point		［備考］両足を踏み換える。挙動**21**・**22**腰の切換え速く。 [Note] Switch positions of both feet. Movements **21** and **22**: Switch the waist quickly.	

96

24 挙 動 Move	25 挙 動 Move
右手刀中段受け。左手刀胸前。	左下段払い。右拳右腰に引く。
Execute a Chudan-Uke with a Right-Shuto. Pull the Left-Shuto to the front of the chest.	Execute a Left-Gedan-Harai. Pull the right fist to the right waist.

東
East

西
East

（西から見る）
Seen from the west.

（㉕〜㉖への動作）
Movement from ㉕ to ㉖.

（西から見る）
Seen from the west.

㉕-A

㉖
左後屈立ち。
Left-Kokutsudachi

㉗
左前屈立ち（半身）。
Left-Zenkutsudachi (Hanmi)

㉗-A

左足の位置そのまま。右足をすり出す。	右脚を軸として後ろへ振り向き前屈立ち。
Maintain the same left foot position. Slide out the right foot.	Pivoting on the right foot, turn back and stand in a Zenkutsudachi.

97

エンピ

26 挙動 Move | 27 挙動 Move

手の動作 Hands

26: 右上段揚げ突き。相手の左上段突きを下から上にはね上げ、相手の顎を突き上げる（甲上向）。左拳左腰に引く。

Execute a Right-Jodan-Age-Tsuki. Fend off the Left-Jodan-Tsuki (from the opponent) by pushing the arm up from the lower side, and push the opponent's jaw up. (The back of the right hand is facing up.) Pull the left fist to the left waist.

27: 右拳開掌・右拳左肩前上、左拳下段突き。

Open the right fist. Place the right fist on the front of the left shoulder. Execute a Gedan-Tsuki with the left fist.

着眼点 Point to see

西 West

（西から見る） Seen from the west.

（㉘〜㉙への動作） Movement from ㉘ to ㉙.

西 West

（西から見る） Seen from the west.

㉘ ／ ㉘−A ／ ㉙ ／ ㉙−A

立ち方 Stance

26: 左前屈立ち（逆半身）。 Left-Zenkutsudachi (Gyaku-Hanmi)

27: 右足前交差立ち。 Kosadachi (right foot in front)

北 North／西 West／東 East／南 South

足の動作 Feet

26: 立ち方はそのまま。
Maintain the same standing position.

27: 右膝を胸前にかい込み、右足で前方正面へ飛び込み右足を屈して体重を支え、左足を右踵の後ろに交差する。

Move the right knee towards the chest. Jump forward with the right foot; bend the right leg forward to support the weight. Move the left leg behind the right ankle so that the legs are crossed.

留意点 Point

26: [備考] 上体をやや左に捻る。
[Note] Slightly twist the upper body to the left.

27: 手の開きと、膝胸前かい込みを同時に行い、左足を右踵の後ろに交差する。

Simultaneously opening the palm and moving the right knee towards the chest, cross the left leg behind the right ankle.

28 挙 動　Move

右下段払い。左拳は左腰に引く。

Execute a Right-Gedan-Harai. Pull the left fist to the left waist.

29 挙 動 Move

左下段払い。右拳は右腰に引く。

Execute a Left-Gedan-Harai. Pull the right fist to the right waist.

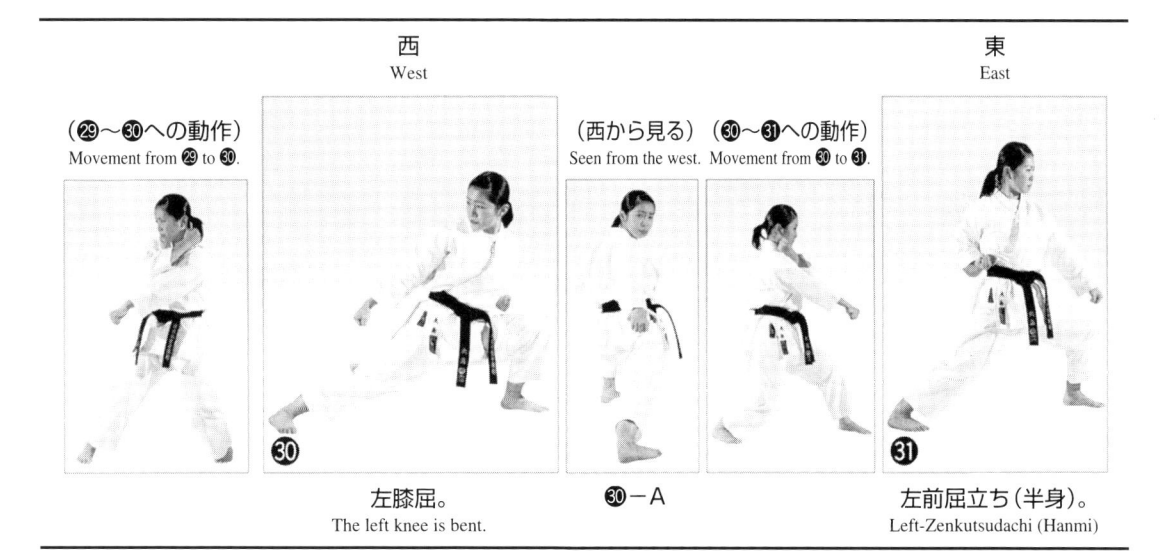

西
West

東
East

（㉙〜㉚への動作）
Movement from ㉙ to ㉚.

（西から見る）（㉚〜㉛への動作）
Seen from the west. Movement from ㉚ to ㉛.

㉚

㉚－A

㉛

左膝屈。
The left knee is bent.

左前屈立ち（半身）。
Left-Zenkutsudachi (Hanmi)

右足の位置はそのまま、左足を一歩後ろへ引き、やや広めに左膝を屈し右膝を伸ばす。

The right foot remains in the same position. Pull the left foot one step. Bend the left knee rather widely and stretch the right knee.

右脚を軸として左足を少し引き気味に左前屈立ち。

Pivoting on the right foot, slightly pull the left foot and stand in a Left-Zenkutsudachi.

エンピ

	30 挙 動 Move	**31** 挙 動 Move
手の動作 Hands	右掌底中段押し上げ受け。腰を左に回転し、掌底を左斜め前方肩の高さ、手首を十分に曲げる（右掌甲下向）。左拳左腰に引く。 Execute a Chudan-Osiage-Uke with the bottom of the right palm. Turn the waist to the left and move the bottom of the palm towards the left side and at shoulder height. Bend the wrist sufficiently. (The back of the right hand faces down.) Pull the left fist to the left waist.	右掌底中段押し上げ受け。左掌底中段押し下げ受け。右掌を右腰前から、左掌を左肩前から同時に動かして右掌底を右肩前へ、手首を下へ十分に曲げる。左掌底を左腰前へ、手首を上へ十分折り曲げ肘を伸ばす。 Execute a Chudan-Oshoage-Uke with the bottom of the right palm. Execute a Chudan-Oshisage-Uke with the bottom of the left palm. Moving the right palm from the front of the right waist and simultaneously moving the left palm from the front of the left shoulder, move the bottom of the right palm to the front of the right shoulder; lower and bend the right wrist sufficiently. Move the bottom of the left palm to the front of the left waist; sufficiently raise and bend the left wrist up. Then stretch the elbow.
着眼点 Point to see	東南 EastSouth	南 South
立ち方 Stance	左前屈立ち。 Left-Zenkutsudachi	右前屈立ち。 Right-Zenkutsudachi
足の動作 Feet	立ち方はそのまま。 Maintain the same standing position.	左足を半歩引き寄せ、右足を前方正面へすり出す。 Pull the left foot a half-step. Slide the right foot forward.
留意点 Point	［備考］ゆっくり力を入れる。 [Note] Slowly exert force.	

32 挙　動　Move

左掌底中段押し上げ受け。右掌底中段押し下げ受け。左掌を左腰前から、右掌を右肩前から同時に動かして、左掌底を左肩前へ、手首を下へ十分折り曲げる。右掌底を右腰前へ、手首を上へ十分折り曲げ肘を伸ばす。

Execute a Chudan-Oshiage-Uke with the bottom of the left palm. Execute a Chudan-Oshisage-Uke with the bottom of the right palm. Moving the left palm from the front of the left waist and simultaneously moving the right palm from the front of the right shoulder, move the bottom of the left palm to the front of the left shoulder; lower and bend the left wrist sufficiently. Move the bottom of the right palm to the front of the right waist; raise and bend the right wrist up sufficiently. Then stretch the elbow.

南
South

（西から見る）
Seen from the west.

（㉝〜㉞への動作）
Movement from ㉝ to ㉞

㉝－A

㉞

（㉞〜㉟への動作）
Movement from ㉞ to ㉟

左前屈立ち。
Left-Zenkutsudachi

左足を前方正面へすり出す。

Slide the left foot forward.

㉛・㉜・㉝挙動。右手と左手は交差しないように。ゆっくり力を込めて手足同時に決まるように。

In Movements ㉛, ㉜ and ㉝, do not cross the right and left hands. Slowly exert force and make the stance with hands and legs at the same time.

エンピ

33 挙動 Move

手の動作 / Hands

右掌底中段押し上げ受け。左掌底中段押し下げ受け。右掌を右腰前から、左掌を左肩前から同時に動かして、右掌底を右肩前へ、手首を下へ十分折り曲げ、左掌底を左腰前へ、手首を上へ十分折り曲げ肘を伸ばす。

Execute a Chudan-Oshiage-Uke with the right palm bottom. Execute a Chudan-Oshisage-Uke with the left palm bottom. Moving the right palm from the front of the right waist and simultaneously moving the left palm from the front of the left shoulder, move the bottom of the right palm to the front of the right shoulder; lower and bend the right wrist sufficiently. Move the bottom of the left palm to the front of the left waist and raise and bend the left wrist up sufficiently. Then stretch the elbow.

着眼点 / Point to see

南 / South

(㉟〜㊱への動作) / Movement from ㉟ to ㊱

㉟

立ち方 / Stance

右前屈立ち。
Right-Zenkutsudachi

足の動作 / Feet

右足を前方正面へすり出す。
Slide the right foot forward.

留意点 / Point

---

34 挙動 Move

手の動作 / Hands

右掌下段払い。右拳を左肩前から、左拳を下から同時に動かして右拳下段払い。左拳左腰に引く。

Execute a Gedan-Harai with the right palm. Moving the right fist from the front of the left shoulder and simultaneously moving the left fist from the lower side, execute a Gedan-Harai with the right fist. Pull the left fist to the left waist.

着眼点 / Point to see

南 / South

(西から見る) / Seen from the west.

㊱　㊱-A

立ち方 / Stance

左後屈立ち。
Left-Kokutsudachi

足の動作 / Feet

腰を左に回転し、左肩を引くようにして上体を左に向け前方正面へ寄足気味。

Rotate the waist to the left. Pulling the left shoulder, turn the upper body to the left and make a slightly forward Yoriashi.

留意点 / Point

右手首を相手の手首に強く打ちつけ、左手を引き抜く。

Hit the opponent's wrist hard using the right wrist and pull the left hand out.

方位 / 北 North, 西 West, 東 East, 南 South

動作の分解 / Kumite in detail

右手と左手は交差しないように、足刀部が床面に密着し、ゆっくりと力を込めて手足が同時に決まることが肝心。

① ② ③

Do not cross the right and left hands. Make sure the feet (Sokuto) are pressed to the floor and you fix both hands and feet simultaneously by exerting force on them slowly.

35 挙動 Move

右掌下段（甲下向）。左掌上段掴み受け（掌斜上向）
右肘を曲げて、右脇腹に引き寄せる。左掌は上に
向けて額前上に。

Execute a Gedan with the right palm (the back of the hand facing down). Execute a Jodan-Tsukami-Uke with the left palm (the palm facing forward and up). Bend the right elbow and pull it to the right side of the abdomen. Turn the left palm upward and hold it in front of the forehead.

36 挙動 Move

右手刀中段受け。両掌を
頭上で右から左へ回し両
足接地と同時に右手刀受
け。左手刀胸前。

Execute a Chudan-Uke with Right-Shuto. Rotate both palms from the right to the left above the head. When both feet land on the ground, execute a Uke with Right-Shuto. Pull the left Shuto to the chest.

南
South

(西から見る)
Seen from the west.

(㊲〜㊳への動作)
Movement from ㊲ to ㊳

南
South

㊲
右足前不動立ち。
Fudodachi (right foot in front)

㊲-A

㊳
左後屈立ち。
Left-Kokutsudachi

前方正面へ寄足。
Step forward with Yoriashi.

左回転飛・気合もろとも両足を高
くかい込み（あぐらをかくように）
高く飛び上がって一回転。

Rotate left and fly (Hidari-Kaiten-Tobi). With a Kiai, scoop the both legs high (as if you were sitting cross-legged), then jump and rotate 360° in a leap.

[備考] 上体はやや前に倒す。

[Note] Bring down the upper half of the body slightly forward.

挙動㉟・㊱は、相手の右上段突きを左前腕で受けながら左手で相手
の襟を掴み、右手を相手の股に入れ両手で相手を肩に担ぎ上げて
投げ飛ばす意味である。

Movements ㉟ and ㊱ are described as "flows": fend off a Right-Jodan-Tuski from the opponent with the left forearm and, at the same time, grabbing the opponent's collar using the left hand, insert the right hand into the opponent's crotch, and lift the opponent onto the shoulders using the both hands; throw the opponent.

気合。
Kiai.

素早く互いに上下に引き絞るように、右拳下段受け左拳上段掴み受け
ようにと同時に、体重を後屈立ちから不動立ちに移動し、右拳で上段掴み不
受けを素早く相手の股に入れ両手で投げ飛ばす。

① ②

By quickly pulling and wringing both hands together up and down, execute a Gedan-Uke with the right fist and pull the left fist towards the left waist. Execute a Jodan-Tsukami-Uke with the left fist and at the same time move your body weight by changing the standing position from a Kokutsudachi to a Fudodachi. Quickly push your right fist into the opponent's crotch and throw the opponent with both hands.

エンピ

		37 挙　動　Move	止　め　Stop
手の動作 Hands		左手刀中段受け。右手刀胸前。 Execute a Chudan-Uke with the Left-Shuto. Pull the right Shuto to the chest.	左掌右拳左腰（左足を引き用意の姿勢に戻る）。 Pull the left palm and right fist to the left waist. (Pull the left foot and return to the Ready position.)
着眼点 Point to see	(㊳〜㊴への動作) Movement from ㊳ to ㊴	南 South ㊴ 右後屈立ち。 Right-Kokutsudachi	（西から見る） Seen from the west. ㊴-A	南 South ㊵ 閉足立ち。 Heisokudachi
立ち方 Stance				
北 North 西 West ─ 東 East 南 South				
足の動作 Feet		右足を一歩引く。 Pull the right foot one step.		閉足立ち。 Heisokudachi
留意点 Point				

直 立 Stand

両手は開いて大腿部両側
に付けて伸ばす。

Open both hands and stretch the arms down to the sides of the thighs.

南
South

㊶

結び立ち。
Musubidachi.

結び立ち。
Musubidachi.

松村ローハイ
マツムラローハイ

[特　徴]

　この形は、鷺足立ちによる蹴りのさばき、開手による中段、下段の流し受け、相手の突きを巻き込んでの投技等に特徴がある。
　連続する技をダイナミック、かつ、スピーディに演武することが要求される。

MATSUMURA ROHAI

[Characteristics]

This Kata is characterized by various wazas; for example, handling a Keri using a Sagiashidachi, blocking a Chudan/Gedan with open hands and taking an opponent's Tsuki in Nagewaza. Using wazas in a series dynamically and with speed is of critical importance.

マツムラローハイ

	直立 Stand	用意 Ready	1 挙動 Move	2 挙動 Move
手の動作 Hands	両手は開き、体の両側に伸ばす。 Open both hands and stretch them on both sides of the body.	両手は開手のまま右甲に左掌を重ねて下腹部前に構える。 Open both hands. Place the left hand on the back of the right hand. Hold them in front of the lower abdomen.	両手は開手のまま、大腿部前に置く。 Open both hands and hold them in front of the thighs.	両手は、開手のまま肩の高さまで上げ、流し受け（平行受け）。 While opening both hands, raise them to shoulder level, and Nagashi-Uke (Heiko-Uke).
着眼点 Point to see	南 South	南 South	南 South	南 South
立ち方 Stance	結び立ち。 Musubidachi	結び立ち。 Musubidachi	八字立ち。 Hachijidachi	八字立ち。 Hachijidachi
北 North / 西 West / 東 East / 南 South			（白から黒へ動く。） (Move from White to Black.)	
足の動作 Feet	結び立ち。 Musubidachi	そのまま。 Maintain the same position.	右足を西へ運び八字立ち。 Move the right foot towards the west and Hachijidachi.	そのまま。 Maintain the same position.
留意点 Point				
動作の分解 Kumite in detail				中段突きを、両手刀にて流し受け。 ① Block a Chudan-Tsuki with a Nagashi-Uke using a Ryo-Shuto.

3 挙動 Move	4 挙動 Move	5 挙動 Move
右手刀下段払い、左開手は水月前に置く。	左手は掛手、右拳は脇へ引く。	右鈎突き、左拳は脇へ引く。
Right-Shuto-Gedan-Harai. Place the open left hand in front of the abdomen.	Left hand is Kakete. Pull the right fist to the side of the body.	Execute a Right-Kagi-Tsuki. Pull the left fist to the side of the body.

（西から見る）
Seen from the west.

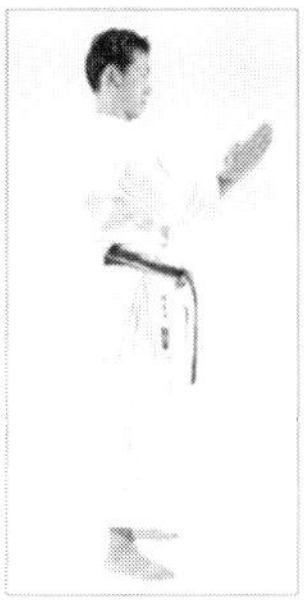

西 West 　　東 East 　　東 East

❹-A 　　❺ 四股立ち。 Shikodachi 　　❻ 左猫足立ち。 Left-Nekoashidachi 　　❼ 四股立ち。 Shikodachi

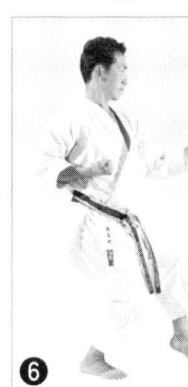

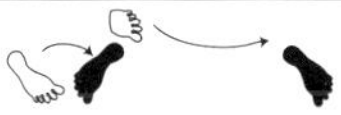

右足を西へ踏み出す。	右足を軸に東へ向き、左足は引く。	左足を東へ大きく踏み出し、右足を少し寄せる。
Move the right foot one step towards the west.	Pivoting on the right foot, turn to the east. Pull the left foot.	Move the left foot wide towards the east. Pull the right foot a little.

鈎突きは、体と平行、水平にし、拳先は体側で止める。鈎突きの時、自然な寄足になる。

Execute a Kagi-Tsuki when the body is parallel and horizontal. Hold the top of the fist on the body side. Kagi-Tsuki is done in a natural Yori-Ashi.

② 中段突き。 Chudan-Tsuki 　　③ 中段蹴りを右手刀払い。 Block a Chudan-Keri with a Right-Shuto-Harai. 　　④ 中段突き。 Chudan-Tsuki 　　⑤ 中段突きを、掛手。 Block a Chudan-Tsuki with a Kakete.

マツムラローハイ

	6 挙動 Move	7 挙動 Move	8 挙動 Move	9 挙動 Move
手の動作 Hands	両拳は握り、脇へ引く。 Hold both fists on the sides of the body.	そのまま。 Maintain the same position.	そのまま。 Maintain the same position.	そのまま。 Maintain the same position.
着眼点 Point to see	東 East	南 South	南 South	南 South
立ち方 Stance	結び立ち。 Musubidachi	結び立ち。 Musubidachi		
足の動作 Feet	左足を右足へ引きつける。 Pull the left foot next to the right foot.	そのまま。 Maintain the same position.	左足を一歩南へ運ぶ。 Move the left foot one step towards the south.	右足を一歩南へ運ぶ。 Move the right foot one step towards the south.
留意点 Point			❾から⓫までは、普通に歩くように運ぶ。 Execute ❾ through ⓫ with nomal walking steps.	
動作の分解 Kumite in detail	腕を捕り、中段突き。 ⑥ Catch the arm and execute a Chudan-Tsuki.			

北 North / 西 West — 東 East / 南 South

10 挙　動　Move	**11** 挙　動　Move
そのまま。	右手刀下段払い。左手は、額の前に構える。
Maintain the same position.	Execute a Right-Shuto-Gedan-Harai. Hold the left hand in front of the forehead.

南	南西
South	Southwest

⑫

⑬

左鷺足立ち。軸足(左足)は、南西に対して45度方向。
Left-Sagiashidachi. The pivoting foot (left foot) is at a 45 degree angle to the southwest.

左足を半歩南へ運ぶ。	左足を北東へ引く。
Move the left foot a half step towards the south.	Pull the left foot towards the northeast.

⑫の左足は、上足底を着けた（踵は上げている）瞬間、動きを止める。	鷺足立ち、右手刀下段払い、左開手の構えは、同時に行う。右足は、大腿部を水平にし、足首を伸ばす。
Stop the movement when the toes of the left foot ⑫ touch the floor (the heel is still in the air).	Simultaneously, execute Sagiashidachi and a Right-Shuto-Gedan-Harai, with the open left palm posing. Raise the right thigh parallel (to the floor) and stretch the right ankle.

111

マツムラローハイ

12 挙動 Move | 13 挙動 Move

手の動作 / Hands

12: 右開手中段外受け、左手は、右小手に添える（中段小手支え受け）。
Execute a Chudan-Soto-Uke with the open right hand. Place the left hand on the right forearm (Chudan-Kote-Sasae-Uke).

13: 右手で巻き込みを行い、左中段横払い。
Execute a Makikomi with the right hand and execute a Left-Chudan-Yoko-Harai.

着眼点 / Point to see

南西 / Southwest

(⑭〜⑮への動作〈巻き込み〉)
Transition from movement ⑭ to movement ⑮ (Makikomi).

南西 / Southwest

立ち方 / Stance

12: 右前屈立ち。 Right-Zenkutsudachi

13: 四股立ち。 Shikodachi

北 North / 西 West / 東 East / 南 South

足の動作 / Feet

12: 右足を南西へ踏みおろす。
Move the right foot one step down towards the southwest.

13: 左足を南西へ踏み出す。
Move the left foot one step to the southwest.

留意点 / Point

12挙動、13挙動は連続して行う。
Move from 12 to 13 continuously.

動作の分解 / Kumite in detail

巻き込みの要領。

Ⓐ The knack of catch (Makikomi). Ⓑ Ⓒ Ⓓ

112

14 挙 動 Move	**15** 挙 動 Move	**16** 挙 動 Move
右拳中段鈎突き、左拳は脇へ引く。	右手刀下段払い、左手は額の前に構える。	右開手中段外受け、左手は右小手に添える（右中段小手支え受け）。
Execute a Chudan-Kagi-Tsuki with the right fist. Pull the left fist to the side of the body.	Execute a Right-Shuto-Gedan-Harai. Hold the left hand in front of the forehead.	Execute a Chudan-Soto-Uke with the open right hand. Place the left hand on the right forearm (Right-Chudan-Kote-Sasae-Uke).
南西 Southwest	南東 Southeast	南東 Southeast
⑯	⑰	⑱
四股立ち。 Shikodachi	左鷺足立ち。 Left-Sagiashidachi	右前屈立ち。 Right-Zenkutsudachi
そのまま。	左足を北西へ引く。	右足を南東へ踏みおろす。
Maintain the same position.	Pull the left foot towards the northwest.	Move the right foot one step down towards the southeast.

16挙動、**17**挙動は連続して行う。（**14**〜**15**への動作〈巻き込み〉と同様の動作を行う。）

Move from **16** to **17** continuously. (Do the same movements shown in Photographs **14** and **15**, Makikomi.)

中段蹴りを、鷺足立ちとなり、手刀下段払い。

⑦ Block a Chudan-Keri with a Shuto-Gedan-Harai in Sagi-ashidachi.

中段突きを、開手中段小手支え受け。

⑧ Block a Chudan-Tsuki with a Chudan-Kote-Sasae-Uke with the open hand.

マツムラローハイ

	17 挙動 Move		18 挙動 Move	
手の動作 Hands	右手で相手の腕を巻き込み脇に引き、左中段横払い。 Catch the opponent's arm (Makikomi) with the right hand, pull the arm to the side of the body and then execute a Left-Chudan-Yoko-Harai.	右中段鉤突き、左拳は脇へ引く。 Execute a Right-Chudan-Kagi-Tsuki. Pull the left fist to the side of the body.	左開手掌底を下方に向け、右体側から。 Execute a Shotei with the open left hand downwards from the right side of the body.	左開手を左体側へ移し。 Move the open left hand to the left side of the body.
着眼点 Point to see	南東 Southeast	南東 Southeast	下方 Down	下方 Down
立ち方 Stance	四股立ち。 Shikodachi	四股立ち。 Shikodachi		
足の動作 Feet	左足を南東へ踏み出す。 Move the left foot one step towards the southeast.	そのまま。 Maintain the same position.	右足を南へ運ぶ。 Move the right foot towards the south.	そのまま。 Maintain the same position.
留意点 Point				
動作の分解 Kumite in detail	⑨ 相手の腕を捕り。 Catch the opponent's arm.	⑩ 相手の右腕を巻き込み、裏突き。 Catch (Makikomi) the opponent's right arm and execute a Ura-Tsuki.	⑪ 左手を後方へ大きく振る。 Swing the left arm all the way back.	⑫ 相手の腕を巻き込み倒す。 Catch (Makikomi) the opponent's arm and bring the opponent down.

(⑳〜㉑への動作)
Movement of ⑳〜㉑.

114

19 挙動 Move	20 挙動 Move	21 挙動 Move	22 挙動 Move
左開手を掬うように上腕へ引き上げながら握り、右拳にて下方へ突く。	右手刀下段払い、左手は額の前に構える。	右開手中段外受け、左手は右小手に添える（右中段小手支え受け）。	右手で相手の腕を巻き込み脇へ引き、左中段横払い。
Raise the open left hand (close the hand at the same time) towards the upper arm and execute a Tsuki with the right fist.	Execute a Right-Shuto-Gedan-Harai. Hold the left hand in front of the forehead.	Execute a Chudan-Soto-Uke with the open right hand. Place the left hand on the right forearm (Right-Chudan-Kote-Sasae-Uke).	Catch(Makikomi) the opponent's arm with the right hand and pull the arm to the side, then execute a Left-Chudan-Yoko-Harai.
下方 Down	南 South	南 South	南 South
㉑	㉒	㉓	㉔
四股立ち。 Shikodachi	左鷺足立ち。 Left-Sagiashidachi	右前屈立ち。 Right-Zenkutsudachi	四股立ち。 Shikodachi
そのまま。	左足を北へ引く。	右足を南へ踏みおろす。	左足を南へ踏み出す。
Maintain the same position.	Pull the left foot towards the north.	Move the right foot one step down towards the south.	Move the left foot towards the south.

㉑挙動、㉒挙動は連続して行う。（⑭～⑮への動作〈巻き込み〉と同様の動作を行う。）

Move from ㉑ to ㉒ continuously. (Do the same movements shown in Photographs ⑭ and ⑮, Makikomi.)

中段突き。

⑬

Execute a Chudan-Tsuki.

マツムラローハイ

	23 挙動 Move	24 挙動 Move	25 挙動 Move	26 挙動 Move
手の動作 Hands	右中段鉤突き、左拳は脇へ引く。 Execute a Right-Chudan-Kagi-Tsuki. Pull the left fist to the side of the body.	両開手にて、下段流し受け。 Execute a Gedan-Nagashi-Uke with open hands.	右拳は脇へ引き、左拳は、甲を上にして水月前に水平に構える（右脇構え）。 Pull the right fist to the side of the body. Hold the left fist (the back of the hand facing up) horizontally in front of the abdomen (Right-Waki-Kamae).	右上段突き、左中段裏突きを同時に行う（双手突き）。 Execute a Right-Jodan-Tsuki and a Left-Chudan-Ura-Tsuki simultaneously (Morote-Tsuki).
着眼点 Point to see	南 South	南 South	南 South	南 South
立ち方 Stance	四股立ち。 Shikodachi	右前屈立ち。 Right-Zenkutsudachi	結び立ち。 Musubidachi	左前屈立ち。 Left-Zenkutsudachi
足の動作 Feet	そのまま。 Maintain the same position.	右足を南へ踏み出す。 Move the right foot towards the south.	右足を左足へ引きつける。 Pull the right foot next to the left foot.	左足を南へ一歩踏み出す。 Move the left foot one step towards the south.
留意点 Point				
動作の分解 Kumite in detail		中段蹴りを、両開手にて流し受け。 ⑭ Block (Nagashi-Uke) a Chudan-Keri with open hands.		上段突きを、双手突き。 ⑮ Block a Jodan-Tsuki with a Morote-Tsuki.

27 挙動 Move	28 挙動 Move	29 挙動 Move	30 挙動 Move
左拳は脇へ引き、右拳は、甲を上にして水月前に水平に構える（左脇構え）。	左上段突き、右中段裏突きを同時に行う（双手突き）。	右拳は脇へ引き、左拳は、甲を上にして水月前に水平に構える（右脇構え）。	右上段突き、左中段裏突きを同時に行う（双手突き）。
Pull the left fist to the side of the body. Hold the right fist (the back of the hand facing up) horizontally in front of the abdomen (Left-Waki-Kamae).	Execute a Left-Jodan-Tsuki and a Right-Chudan-Ura-Tsuki simultaneously (Morote-Tsuki).	Pull the right fist to the side of the body. Hold the left fist (the back of the hand facing up) horizontally in front of the abdomen (Right-Waki-Kamae).	Execute a Right-Jodan-Tsuki and a Left-Chudan-Ura-Tsuki simultaneously (Morote-Tsuki).
南 South	南 South	南 South	南 South
㉙	㉚	㉛	㉜
結び立ち。 Musubidachi	右前屈立ち。 Right-Zenkutsudachi	結び立ち。 Musubidachi	左前屈立ち。 Left-Zenkutsudachi
左足を右足へ引きつける。	右足を一歩南へ踏み出す。	右足を左足へ引きつける。	左足を南へ一歩踏み出す。
Pull the left foot next to the right foot.	Move the right foot one step towards the south.	Pull the right foot next to the left foot.	Move the left foot one step towards the south.

マツムラローハイ

	31 挙動 Move	32 挙動 Move	33 挙動 Move
手の動作 Hands	左中段手刀受け、右拳は脇へ引く。 Execute a Left-Chudan-Shuto-Uke. Pull the right fist to the side of the body.	そのまま。 Maintain the same position.	右中段手刀受け、左掌は掌を上にして水月前に構える。 Execute a Right-Chudan-Shuto-Uke. Hold the left palm (the palm of the hand facing up) in front of the abdomen.
着眼点 Point to see	南 South	南 South	南 South
立ち方 Stance	左猫足立ち。 Left-Nekoashidachi		右猫足立ち。 Right-Nekoashidachi
足の動作 Feet	両足を後ろへ引く。 Pull both feet back.	右中段蹴り。右足裏を左掌に当てる。 Right-Chudan-Keri. The back of the right foot touches the left palm.	左足を後方（北）へ引き。 Pull the left foot back (north).
留意点 Point		蹴りの時、左掌を上下しないこと。 Do not swing the left palm up and down when executing Keri.	㉞の蹴りから㉟の右猫足立ち手刀受けをするまで、左回りで360度回転する。 Turn 360 degrees left from the Keri ㉞ position to the Right-Nekoashidachi ㉟ position, executing a Shuto-Uke.
動作の分解 Kumite in detail	中段突きを、手刀受け。⑯ Block a Chudan-Tsuki with a Shuto-Uke.	中段蹴り。⑰ Execute a Chudan-Keri.	

(㉞〜㉟への動作)
Movement of ㉞〜㉟.

北 North / 西 West / 東 East / 南 South

34 挙動 Move	止め Stop	直立 Stand
左中段手刀受け、右開手は、掌を上にして水月前に構える。 Execute a Left-Chudan-Shuto-Uke. Hold the open right hand (the palm of the hand facing up) in front of the abdomen.	両手は開手のまま右甲に左掌を重ねて下腹部前に構える。 Open both hands, and place the left palm on the back of the right hand and hold them in front of the lower abdomen.	両手をそれぞれ体の両側に伸ばす。 Stretch both hands to the sides of the body.
南 South	南 South	南 South
㊱	㊲	㊳
左猫足立ち。 Left-Nekoashidachi	結び立ち。 Musubidachi	結び立ち。 Musubidachi
右足を大きく引く。 Pull the right foot all the way back.	左足を右足へ引きつける。 Pull the left foot next to the right foot.	そのまま。 Maintain the same position.

二十八歩
ニーパイポ

[特　徴]

　この形は、中国拳法の流れを汲むものであり、身体の屈伸や円運動等による体捌き、受けからの肘固め、双手突き、一本拳の突き等の技法に特徴がある。
　これら攻防の技を敏捷に、また緩急の動作をリズミカルに演武することが要求される。

NIPAIPO

[Characteristics]

NIPAIPO is descended from Chinese martial arts (Chugoku Kempo) and has many effective body movement techniques: stretching and circular movements, when in defense; elbow locks, when pushing; Morote-Tsuki and Ipponken.
It is necessary that defensive and offensive techniques flow quickly, rhythmically quick and slow.

ニーパイポ

	直　立　Stand	用　意　Ready	**1** 挙　動　Move	
手の動作 Hands	両手は開き、体の両側に伸ばす。 Open both hands and stretch them on both sides of the body.	両手は、開手のまま右甲に左掌を重ねて下腹部前に構える。 Open both hands. Place the left hand on the back of the right hand. Hold them in front of the lower abdomen.	両拳は下腹部前に構える。 Hold fists in front of lower abdomen.	
着眼点 Point to see	南 South	南 South	南 South	（東から見る） Seen from the east.
立ち方 Stance	❶ 結び立ち。 Musubidachi	❷ 結び立ち。 Musubidachi	❸ 平行立ち（肩幅）。 Heikodachi (shoulder width)	❸−A
北 North 西 West ─ 東 East 南 South			（白から黒へ動く。） (Move from White to Black.)	
足の動作 Feet	結び立ち。 Musubidachi	そのまま。 Maintain the same position.	左足を北へ引き爪先を東方へ、右足は、左足と平行になるよう上足底を軸に捻る。 Pull left foot back towards north. Pivot toes to east. Twist the right foot pivoting the ball so that the right foot and left foot are parallel.	
留意点 Point				
動作の分解 Kumite in detail				

2 挙動 Move	3 挙動 Move	4 挙動 Move
右拳は甲を下にして右脇に引き、同時に左掌を右正拳に添える。	左掌を右正拳に添えたまま、左脇体側まで引く(このとき右拳は縦にする)。	右中段外受け、左掌は右拳槌部に添える(右中段拳支え受け)。
Pull right fist to right side of body with back of the right hand facing down; at the same time place the left palm beside the right fist.	While placing the left palm on the right fist, pull both arms to the left side of the body (turn the right fist up).	Right-Chudan-Soto-Uke. Place the left palm on the right Kentsui (Right-Chudan-Ken-Sasae-Uke).

南 South	南 South	(東から見る) Seen from the east.	南 South
❹	❺	❺-A	❻
平行立ち。 Heikodachi	平行立ち。 Heikodachi		右猫足立ち。 Right-Nekoashidachi

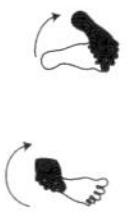

そのまま。	そのまま。		左足上足底を軸にして右足を少し北へ引く。
Maintain the same position.	Maintain the same position.		Pivoting on the ball of left foot, pull the right foot back a little towards the north.

■挙動から❺挙動まで、ゆっくり連続して行う。

Move slowly and continuously from Movement ■ to ❺.

裏打ち。 中段突きを、拳支え受け。

① Block a Chudan-Tsuki with a Ken-Sasae-Uke.

② Ura-Uchi

ニーパイポ

	5 挙動 Move	6 挙動 Move	7 挙動 Move	8 挙動 Move
手の動作 Hands	両拳は下腹部前に構える。 Hold both fists in front of the lower abdomen.	左手は、大きく円を描きながら水月前に掌底受け。右一本拳にて突く。 Turn the left hand in a large circular motion. Shotei-Uke in front of the abdomen. Execute a Right-Ipponken.	左開手にて上段差し手、右拳（一本拳）は脇へ引く。 Jodan-Sashite with the left palm open. Pull the right fist (Ippon-ken) to the right side of the body.	左掌を頚部の高さに下げ、右拳槌（一本拳）にて打つ。 Lower the left fist to neck height and execute a Right-Kentsui (Ipponken).
着眼点 Point to see	南 South	西 West	南東 Southeast	南東 Southeast
立ち方 Stance	平行立ち。 Heikodachi	四股立ち。 Shikodachi	左基立ち。 Left-Motodachi	左基立ち。 Left-Motodachi
足の動作 Feet	左足上足底を軸にして東方へ爪先を向け、右足を東方へ少し出す。 Pivoting on the ball of the left foot, pivot the toes towards east and push out with the right foot to the east.	左足を東へ一歩運ぶ。 Move one step towards the east with the left foot.	左足を南西へ引く。 Pull the left foot towards the southwest.	そのまま。 Maintain the same position.
留意点 Point		掌底受けと一本拳は同時に行う。 Shotei-Uke and an Ipponken simultaneously.	左差し手を行うとき、体は半身（写真❾参照）になること。 When executing a Left-Sashite, the body becomes Hanmi (See the photo).	
動作の分解 Kumite in detail		③ 中段突きを、掌底で受け、同時に一本拳にて突く。 Block a Chudan-Tsuki with a Shotei and simultaneously execute an Ipponken.	④ 上段突きを、差し手で受け。 Block Jodan-Tsuki with a Sashite.	⑤ 拳槌にて打つ。 Hit with a Kentsui.

North / West / East / South

9 挙動 Move	10 挙動 Move	11 挙動 Move	12 挙動 Move
右手は一本拳のまま中段肘当て（右手甲は上にする）。 Keep the right hand in an Ipponken and execute a Chudan-Hijiate (the back of the hand facing up).	南へ右一本拳（縦突き）で突く。 Right-Ipponken (Tate-Tsuki) towards the south.	左中段突き、右拳は脇へ引く。 Left-Chudan-Tsuki. Pull right fist to the right side of the body.	右中段内受け（右中段横打ち）、左拳は脇へ引く。 Right-Chudan-Uchi-Uke (Right-Chudan-Yoko-Uchi). Pull left fist to the left side of the body.
南 South ⑪ 四股立ち。 Shikodachi	南 South ⑫ 左片足で立つ。 Stand on the left foot.	南 South ⑬ 右基立ち。 Right-Motodachi	南 South ⑭ 四股立ち。 Shikodachi
右足を南へ踏み出す。 Move the right foot one step towards the south.	左足を軸にして、南へ右中段蹴り。 Pivoting on the left foot, execute a Right-Chudan-Keri towards the south.	右足を踏みおろす。 Put down the right foot.	左足を北へ引く。 Pull the left foot towards the north.
	右一本拳突きと右中段蹴りは同時に行う。 Right-Ipponken and a Right-Chudan-Keri simultaneously.		
踏み込んで肘当て。 ⑥ Step in and execute a Hijiate.	上段突きを、一本拳にて突き受け、同時に中段蹴り。 ⑦ Block a Jodan-Tsuki with an Ipponken; at the same time execute a Chudan-Keri.	中段突き。 ⑧ Chudan-Tsuki	中段突きを、中段内受け（横打ち）。 ⑨ Block a Chudan-Tsuki with a Chudan-Uchi-Uke (Yokouchi).

125

ニーパイポ

	13 挙動 Move	14 挙動 Move	15 挙動 Move
手の動作 Hands	両拳は、甲を上にして双手突き。 Morote-Tsuki with the back of both hands facing upwards.	両拳を胸の前に引き寄せ肘固め。 Pull both fists towards the chest and execute a Hiji-gatame.	左開手にて上段差し手、右拳（一本拳）は脇へ引く。 Jodan-Sashite with the open left palm. Pull the right fist (Ipponken) to the right side of the body.
着眼点 Point to see	南 South	南 South	南東 Southeast
立ち方 Stance	右基立ち。 Right-Motodachi	四股立ち。 Shikodachi	左基立ち。 Left-Motodachi
足の動作 Feet	左足を南へ引き寄せ。 Pull the left foot towards south.	左足を引く。 Pull back the left foot.	左足を南東へ踏み出す。 Move the left foot one step to the southeast.

方位：北 North／西 West／東 East／南 South

留意点 Point

⓫の四股立ち、右肘当てから⓰の四股立肘固めまで、連続して個々に技を極め、肘当て、突き以外の手技は丸みをもたせ、リズミカルな動作をすること。

From ⓫ Shikodachi and Right-Hijiate to ⓰ Shikodachi-Hijigatame, execute wazas continuously. Execute tewazas except Hijiate and Tsuki smoothly and rhythmically.

動作の分解 Kumite in detail

⑩ 双手突き。
Morote-Tsuki.

⑪ 中段突きを、両腕で受け。
Block a Chudan-Tsuki with both arms.

⑫ 両腕で肘固め。
Execute a Hijigatame with both arms.

⑬ 上段突きを、差し手で受け。
Block a Jodan-Tsuki with a Sashite.

16 挙動 Move	17 挙動 Move	18 挙動 Move	19 挙動 Move
左掌を頸部の高さに下げ、右拳槌（一本拳）にて打つ。 Lower the left palm to neck height. Execute (hit) a Right-Kentsui (Ipponken).	両拳、両肘を締めながら上段輪受け。 Closing both fists and bringing both elbows together, execute a Jodan-Wa-Uke.	両拳を胸の前に引き寄せ肘固め。 Pull both fists towards the chest and execute a Hijigatame.	左上段揚げ受け、右拳（一本拳）は脇へ引く。 Left-Jodan-Age-Uke. Pull the right fist (Ipponken) to the right side of the body.
南東 Southeast	北西 Northwest	北西 Northwest	南 South
左基立ち。 Left-Motodachi	右前屈立ち。 Right-Zenkutsudachi	四股立ち。 Shikodachi	左前屈立ち。 Left-Zenkutsudachi
そのまま。 Maintain the same position.	右足を北へ運ぶ。 Move the right foot towards the north.	前屈立ちの位置で四股立ちになる。 Shikodachi at the Zenkutsudachi position.	四股立ちから南へ前屈立ちになる。 From Shikodachi to Zenkutsudachi towards the south.

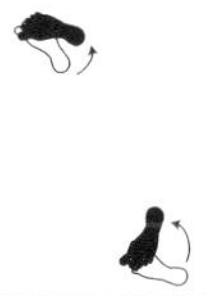

上段輪受けのとき、肘を曲げること。両拳の間隔は、拳一握り分を開ける。

Bend the elbows when executing a Jodan-Wa-Uke. The space between both fists should be about the size of one fist.

⑭ 相手の腕を捕り、一本拳にて突く。
Catching the opponent's arm, execute an Ipponken.

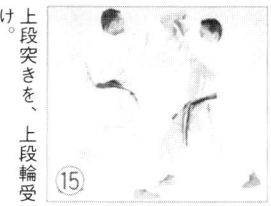

⑮ 上段突きを、上段輪受け。
Block a Jodan-Tsuki with a Jodan-Wa-Uke.

⑯ 中段突きを、両腕で受け、肘固め。
Block a Chudan-Tsuki with both arms and execute a Hijigatame.

⑰ 上段突きを、上段揚げ受け。
Block a Jodan-Tsuki with a Jodan-Age-Uke.

ニーパイポ

	20 挙動 Move	21 挙動 Move	22 挙動 Move
手の動作 Hands	右一本拳（縦）で下方へ突く。左拳は右上腕へ添える。 Right-Ipponken (vertical). Place the left fist on the right upper arm.	右一本拳は、甲を前方に向け右肩上方に上げる。左拳は、右上腕に添えたまま。 Turn the back of a Right-Ipponken towards the front and raise it above the right shoulder. The left fist should stay on the right upper arm.	右手刀下段払い、左開手にて、右肩近くへ引く。 Right-Shuto-Gedan-Harai. Pull the left open palm towards the right shoulder.
着眼点 Point to see	下方 Down	南 South	西 West
立ち方 Stance		右基立ち。 Right-Motodachi	左猫足立ち。 Left-Nekoashidachi
足の動作 Feet	前屈立ちから、右足を送り膝を床へ付ける。 From a Zenkutsudachi, move the right foot and lower the knee so it touches the floor.	右足を南へ一歩踏み出し、左足も少し南へ寄せる。 Move the right foot one step towards the south. Move the left foot a little towards the south.	左足を西へ運び。 Move the left foot to the west.
留意点 Point			
動作の分解 Kumite in detail	一本拳にて突く。 Execute an Ipponken.	突くと同時に、相手の股へ腕を入れる。 While executing an Ipponken, thrust the arm between the opponent's inner thighs.	持ち上げて、後方へ投げる。 Lift and throw the body backwards.

23 挙 動 Move	24 挙 動 Move
左手刀下段払い、右開手は掌を上にして水月前に引く。	左中段外受け、右拳は掌を外にして、前額部に構える。
Left-Shuto-Gedan-Harai. Pull the right open palm (the hollow of the hand facing up) to the abdomen.	Left-Chudan-Soto-Uke. Place the right fist (the palm facing out) in front of forehead.

西
West

（西から見る）
Seen from the west

㉔－A

㉕

左猫足立ち。
Left-Nekoashidachi

（西から見る）
Seen from the west

㉕－A

西
West

㉖

左猫足立ち。
Left-Nekoashidachi

（北から見る）
Seen from the north.

㉖－A

そのまま。	そのまま。
Maintain the same position.	Maintain the same position.

ニーパイポ

	25 挙 動 Move	26 挙 動 Move
手の動作 Hands	右中段外受け、左拳は前額部に構える。 Right-Chudan-Soto-Uke. Place the left fist in front of forehead.	両開手は、体の左右で掛手を行う。 Open both palms and execute a Kakete on both sides of the body.
着眼点 Point to see	東 East （北から見る） Seen from the north. ㉗　㉗－A 右猫足立ち。 Right-Nekoashidachi.	北 North （北から見る） Seen from the north. ㉘　㉘－A 左鷺足立ち。 Left-Sagiashidachi.
立ち方 Stance		
足の動作 Feet	右足を南へ寄せ。 Move the right foot towards the south.	体を北へ向け、鷺足立ち。この時、左膝の裏へ右足甲を付ける。 Shift the body towards the north. Sagiashidachi. Place the front of the right foot behind and against the back of the left knee.
留意点 Point		
動作の分解 Kumite in detail		㉑ 中段突きを、左掛手で捕り。 Catch a Chudan-Tsuki with a Left-Kakete. ㉒ 更に中段突きを、右掛手で捕り。 Then, catch a Chudan-Tsuki with a Right-Kakete.

130

27 挙 動 Move

右開手は甲を上にして上側、左開手は甲を下にして下側へ、掌面を合わせて水月前に構える。

Turn the right open hand up. (The back of the hand facing up). Turn the left open hand down. (The back of the hand facing down). Close both palms together, and hold them in front of the abdomen.

北
North

（北から見る）
Seen from the north.

㉙
左基立ち。
Left-Motodachi

㉙-A

右足を南へ一歩引き。

Pull the right foot one step towards the south.

28 挙 動 Move

両掌（右手上、左手下）を重ねたまま、前方へ伸ばす。

Hold both palms (right hand above, left hand below) apart and parallel to each other, then extend them forward.

北西
Northwest

（北から見る）
Seen from the north.

㉚
左基立ち。
Left-Motodachi

㉚-A

両足は北西へ寄足。

Pull both feet towards the northwest.

㉙から㉛まで連続して行う。

Execute from ㉙ to ㉛ continuously.

㉓ 中段蹴り。
Chudan-Keri

㉔ 中段突きを、左掌で掬い受け、右手は相手の手首を捕らえ。
Scoop and block a Chudan-Tsuki with the left palm and catch the opponent's wrist with the right hand.

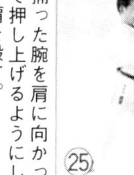

㉕ 捕った腕を肩に向かって押し上げるようにして肩を殺す。
Disable opponent's shoulder by thrusting up his arm against the shoulder.

ニーパイポ

29 挙 動 Move

手の動作 Hands

伸ばした両開手を水月前に引き戻す。

Pull back both open palms to the abdomen.

左開手を上、右開手を下に両掌底を合わせて水月前に構える。

Place the left open palm on the top of the right open palm. Palm bottoms facing each other, hold them in front of the abdomen.

着眼点 Point to see

北西
Northwest

（北西から見る）
Seen from the northwest.

北東
Northeast

（北東から見る）
Seen from the northeast.

㉛　　㉛－A　　㉜　　㉜－A

立ち方 Stance

左基立ち。
Left-Motodachi

右基立ち。
Right-Motodachi

北 North / 西 West / 東 East / 南 South

足の動作 Feet

そのまま。

Maintain the same position.

両上足底を軸に捻り両爪先を北東へ向ける。

Pivoting on the balls of both feet, swivel so that the toes are pointing towards the northeast.

留意点 Point

㉜から㉞まで連続して行う。

Execute from ㉜ to ㉞ continuously.

30 挙　動　Move

両掌（左手上、右手下）を重ねたまま、前方へ伸ばす。

With both palms facing each other, extend them forward (left hand above, right hand below).

伸ばした両開手を水月前に引き戻す。

Pull the extended open palms towards the abdomen.

北東
Northeast

（北東から見る）
Seen from the northeast.

㉝

右基立ち。
Right-Motodachi

㉝－A

北東
Northeast

（北東から見る）
Seen from the northeast.

㉞

右基立ち。
Right-Motodachi

㉞－A

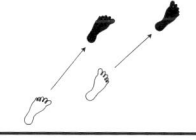

両足は北東へ寄足。

Move both feet towards the northeast.

そのまま。

Maintain the same position.

133

ニーパイポ

31 挙 動　Move

手の動作 / Hands

両掌（左手上、右手下）を重ねたまま、前方へ伸ばす。

With both palms facing each other, extend them forward (left hand above, right hand below).

伸ばした両開手を水月前に引き戻す。

Pull the extended open palms towards the abdomen.

着眼点 / Point to see

北　North

（北から見る）
Seen from the north.

㉟

㉟－A

北　North

（北から見る）
Seen from the north.

㊱

㊱－A

立ち方 / Stance

右基立ち。
Right-Motodachi

右基立ち。
Right-Motodachi

北 North / 西 West / 東 East / 南 South

足の動作 / Feet

両足は、北へ寄足。

Move both feet towards the north.

そのまま。

Maintain the same position.

留意点 / Point

㉟と㊱は連続して行う。

Execute ㉟ and ㊱ continuously.

動作の分解 / Kumite in detail

32 挙動 Move	33 挙動 Move	34 挙動 Move	35 挙動 Move
右手刀を頭上から大きく振って、前方中段に打ち落とし、左開手は脇へ引く。	左手刀を頭上から大きく振って、前方中段に打ち落とし、右開手は脇へ引く。	右四本貫手で突く。左開手は、甲を外にして水月前に構える。	左手刀を頭上から大きく振って、前方中段に打ち落とし、右開手は脇へ引く。
Execute a Right-Shuto from over the head down to a front Chudan. Pull the open left palm to the side of the body.	Execute a Left-Shuto from over the head down to a front Chudan. Pull the open right palm to the side of the body.	Strike with a Right-Yonhon-Nukite. Hold the left open palm (back of the hand facing out) in front of the abdomen.	Execute a Left-Shuto from over the head down to a front Chudan. Pull the right open palm to the side of the body.
南 South	南 South	南 South	南 South
㊲	㊳	㊴	 ㊵
左基立ち。 Left-Motodachi	右基立ち。 Right-Motodachi	四股立ち。 Shikodachi	左基立ち。 Left-Motodachi
右足を西へ運び、南へ向く。	右足を南へ踏み出す。	右足を南へ踏み出す。	左足を南へ踏み出す。
Move the right foot towards the west and face south.	Move the right foot one step towards the south.	Move the right foot one step towards the south.	Move the left foot one step towards the south.

33挙動と34挙動は連続して行う。

Execute Movements 33 and 34 continuously.

㉖ 中段突きを。 
Watch for a Chudan-Tsuki.

㉗ 手刀で打ち落として、受け。  
Strike off and block the Chudan-Tsuki with a Shuto.

㉘ 更に中段突きを。 
Then, for another Chudan-Tsuki.

135

ニーパイポ

	36 挙動 Move	37 挙動 Move	38 挙動 Move	
手の動作 Hands	右手刀を頭上から大きく振って、前方中段に打ち落とし、左開手は脇へ引く。 Execute a Right-Shuto from over the head down to a front Chudan. Pull the left open palm to the side of the body.	左四本貫手で突く。右開手は甲を外にして、水月前に構える。 Strike with a Left-Yonhon-Nukite. Hold the right open palm (back of the hand facing out) in front of the abdomen.	左掌は中段押え受け、右一本拳にて中段突き（左開手は、甲を上にし、右上腕に添える）。 Block a Chudan-Osae-Uke with the left palm. Execute a Chudan-Tsuki with a Right Ipponken. (Place the left open palm, the back of the hand facing up, under the upper right arm.)	
着眼点 Point to see	南 South	南 South	北西 Northwest	（北東から見る） Seen from the northeast.
立ち方 Stance	左基立ち。 Left-Motodachi	四股立ち。 Shikodachi	右基立ち。 Right-Motodachi	㊸-A
足の動作 Feet	そのまま。 Maintain the same position.	左足を南へ踏み出す。 Move the left foot towards the south.	両足を北西へ大きく寄足。 Move both feet wide towards the northwest.	
留意点 Point	㉟挙動から㊲挙動は、連続して行う。 Execute from Movement ㉟ to ㊲ continuously.			
動作の分解 Kumite in detail	手刀で打ち落として、受け。 Strike off and block with a Shuto.	縦四本貫手にて中段突き。 Chudan-Tsuki with Tate-Yonhon-Nukite.	中段突きを、左掌にて押え受け。 Hold and block a Chudan-Tsuki with the left palm.	縦一本拳にて中段突き。 Chudan-Tsuki with Tate-Ipponken.

39 挙 動 Move	40 挙 動 Move	41 挙 動 Move
左掬い受け、右一本拳にて下段へ突く。 Left-Sukui-Uke. Strike down with a Right Ipponken.	左開手にて上段差し手、右拳（一本拳）は脇へ引く。 Open the left palm and Jodan-Sashite. Pull the right fist (Ipponken) to the side of the body.	左掌を頚部の高さに下げ、右拳槌（一本拳）にて打つ。 Lower the left palm to neck height and strike with a Right-Kentsui (Ipponken).
北西 Northwest	南東 Southeast	南東 Southeast
㊹ （北から見る）Seen from the north. ㊹-A 右基立ち。 Right-Motodachi	㊺ 左基立ち。 Left-Motodachi	㊻
更に両足を北西へ大きく寄足。 Move both feet wide further northwest.	左足を北東へ運び。 Move the left foot towards the northeast.	右中段蹴り。 Right-Chudan-Keri
38挙動と39挙動は連続して行う。 Execute Movements 38 and 39 continuously.	40挙動から43挙動は、連続して行う。 Execute from Movement 40 to 43 continuously.	

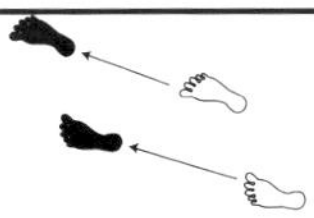

中段突きを、左掌にて掬い受け。

㉝ Scoop and block a Chudan-Tsuki with the left palm.

縦一本拳にて下段突き。

㉞ Gedan-Tsuki with Tate-Ipponken.

ニーパイポ

	42 挙動 Move	43 挙動 Move	44 挙動 Move	
手の動作 Hands	左掌は中段押え受け、右一本拳にて中段突き（左開手は、甲を上にし、右上腕に添える）。 The left palm is Chudan-Osae-Uke. Chudan-Tsuki with Right Ipponken (Hold the left open palm with the back of the hand on top and place the left palm on the right upper arm).	左手は右肩前に掬い受け、右一本拳にて下段へ突く。 Sukui-Uke with the left hand in front of the right shoulder. Right-Ipponken downward.	左肘繰り受け、右拳は脇へ引く。 Left-Hiji-Kuri-Uke. Pull the right fist to the side of the body.	
着眼点 Point to see	南東 Southeast ㊼	南東 Southeast ㊽	北 North ㊾	（北から見る） Seen from the north. ㊾－A
立ち方 Stance	右基立ち。 Right-Motodachi	右基立ち。 Right-Motodachi	左前屈立ち。 Left-Zenkutsudachi	
北 North / 西 West / 東 East / 南 South				
足の動作 Feet	蹴った右足を大きく前に踏み出し、左足を寄せる。 Move the right foot (kicked) wide forward, then pull the left foot forward.	南東へ大きく寄足。 Move both feet wide towards the southeast.	左足を西へ少し寄せ。 Move the left foot a little to the west.	
留意点 Point				
動作の分解 Kumite in detail				

45 挙 動 Move

右下段払い、左拳は脇へ引く。

Right-Gedan-Harai. Pull the left fist to the side of the body.

北
North

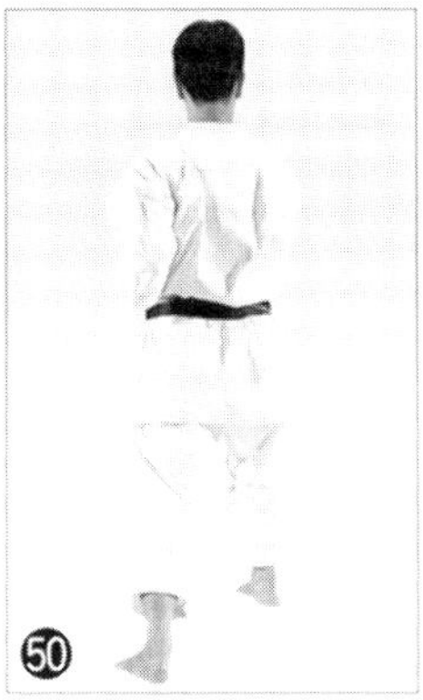

右前屈立ち。
Right-Zenkutsudachi

(北から見る)
Seen from the north.

(50)−A

右足を北へ踏み出す。

Move the right foot one step towards the north.

中段突きを、下段払い。

Block Chudan-Tsuki with Gedan-Harai.

46 挙 動 Move

左中段蹴りが当たる時、右手を開き、中段に置く。

When a Left-Chudan-Keri hits, open the right hand and hold it in a Chudan.

北
North

(北から見る)
Seen from the north.

(51)−A

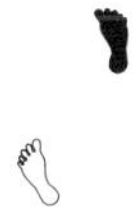

左中段蹴りを右掌に当てる。

Left-Chudan-Keri touches the right palm.

中段蹴り。

Chudan-Keri

ニーパイポ

	47 挙 動 Move	**48** 挙 動 Move
手の動作 Hands	左肘（縦）にて右掌に当てる。 Hold the left elbow (vertical) with the right hand.	右肘繰り受け、左拳は脇へ引く。 Right-Hiji-Kuri-Uke. Pull the left fist to the side of the body.
着眼点 Point to see	北 North　　　　　（北から見る） 　　　　　　　　　Seen from the north. ㊵　　　　　　　㊵－A	北 North　　　　　（北から見る） 　　　　　　　　　Seen from the north. ㊷　　　　　　　㊷－A
立ち方 Stance	右前屈立ち。 Right-Zenkutsudachi	右前屈立ち。 Right-Zenkutsudachi
足の動作 Feet	蹴った左足は、南へ引く。 Pull the left foot (kicked) to the south.	そのまま。 Maintain the same position.
留意点 Point	中段肘当ては、体の中心へ行う。 Execute Chudan-Hijiate to the center of the body.	
動作の分解 Kumite in detail	縦肘当て。 ㊲ Tate-Hijiate	中段突きを、肘繰り受け。 ㊳ Block a Chudan-Tsuki with a Hiji-Kuri-Uke.

北 North　西 West　東 East　南 South

49 挙　動　Move	**50** 挙　動　Move
左下段払い、右拳は脇へ引く。	蹴りが当たる時、左手を開き、中段に置く。
Left-Gedan-Harai. Pull the right fist to the side of the body.	When hit, open the left hand and hold it in a Chudan.

北
North

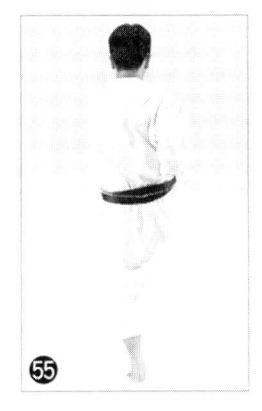

（北から見る）
Seen from the north.

北
North

（北から見る）
Seen from the north.

㊴

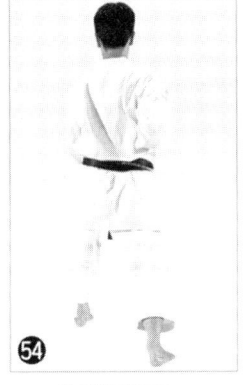

左前屈立ち。
Left-Zenkutsudachi

㊴-A

㊵

㊵-A

左足を北へ一歩踏み出す。

Move the left foot one step towards the north.

右中段蹴りは左掌に当てる。

Right-Chudan-Keri touches the left palm.

ニーパイポ

	51 挙 動 Move	**52** 挙 動 Move
手の動作 Hands	右肘（縦）にて左掌に当てる。 Hold the right elbow (vertical) with the left palm.	右中段外受け、左拳は脇へ引く。 Right-Chudan-Soto-Uke. Pull the left fist to the side of the body.
着眼点 Point to see	北 North　　（北から見る） Seen from the north. ㊱　　　　　㊱－A	北 North　　（北から見る） Seen from the north. ㊲　　　　　㊲－A
立ち方 Stance	左前屈立ち。 Left-Zenkutsudachi	右基立ち。 Right-Motodachi
足の動作 Feet	蹴った右足は、南へ引く。 Pull the right foot (kicked) to the south.	右足を北へ踏み出す。 Move the right foot one step towards the north.
留意点 Point	中段肘当ては、体の中心へ行う。 Execute a Chudan-Hijiate to the center of the body.	
動作の分解 Kumite in detail	肘当て。 ㊴ Hijiate	

53 挙 動 Move

左中段突き、右拳は脇へ引く。

Left-Chudan-Tuski. Pull the right fist to the side of the body.

北
North

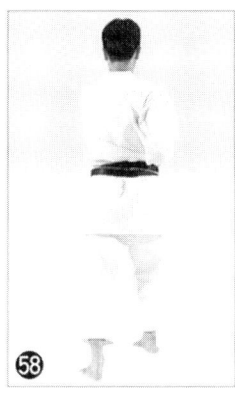

⑱

右基立ち。
Right-Motodachi

⑱－A

（北から見る）
Seen from the north.

そのまま。

Maintain the same position.

54 挙 動 Move

左中段外受け、右拳は脇へ引く。

Left-Chudan-Soto-Uke. Pull the right fist to the side of the body.

北
North

⑲

左基立ち。
Left-Motodachi

⑲－A

（北から見る）
Seen from the north.

左足を北へ踏み出す。

Move the left foot one step towards the north.

ニーパイポ

	55 挙 動 Move	56 挙 動 Move
手の動作 Hands	右中段突き、左拳は脇へ引く。 Right-Chudan-Tsuki. Pull the left fist to the side of the body.	両拳は甲を上にして双手突き。 The back of both fists are facing up and Morote-Tsuki.
着眼点 Point to see	北 North　　（北から見る）Seen from the north. ⑥⓪　　　　　　　　⑥⓪-A	北 North　　（北から見る）Seen from the north. ⑥①　　　　　　　　⑥①-A
立ち方 Stance	左基立ち。 Left-Motodachi	右猫足立ち。 Right-Nekoashidachi
北 North／西 West／東 East／南 South		
足の動作 Feet	そのまま。 Maintain the same position.	右足を北へ大きく踏み出し、左足も寄せる。 Move the right foot wide towards the north. Pull the left foot as well.
留意点 Point		

57 挙 動 Move	58 挙 動 Move	59 挙 動 Move
両拳を胸の前に引き寄せ肘固め。	左掌に右拳槌部分を添え、左脇へ構える。	右中段外受け、左掌は右拳槌部に支える（右中段拳支え）。
Pull both fists to the chest, Hijigatame.	Place a Right-Kentsui on the left palm and hold both hands on the left side of the body.	Right-Chudan-Soto-Uke. Place the left palm on a Right-Kentsui. (Right Chudan-Ken-Sasae)

北 North	（北から見る） Seen from the north.	南 South	南 South
⑫	⑫-A	⑬	⑭
右猫足立ち。 Right-Nekoashidachi		左猫足立ち。 Left-Nekoashidachi	左猫足立ち。 Left-Nekoashidachi

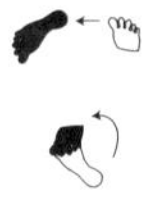

そのまま。	右足を西へ運び、南へ向く。	そのまま。
Maintain the same position.	Move the right foot towards the west and face south.	Maintain the same position.

ニーパイポ

	止め Stop	直立 Stand
手の動作 Hands	両手は、開手にして、右甲に左掌を重ねて下腹部前に構える。 Open both hands, and place the left palm on the back of the right hand and hold them in front of the lower abdomen.	両手をそれぞれ体の両側に伸ばす。 Stretch both hands to the sides of the body.
着眼点 Point to see	南 South ⑥⑤ 結び立ち。 Musubidachi	南 South ⑥⑥ 結び立ち。 Musubidachi
立ち方 Stance		
北 North 西 West ― 東 East 南 South		
足の動作 Feet	左足を右足へ引きつける。 Pull the left foot next to the right foot.	そのまま。 Maintain the same position.
留意点 Point		

146

ニーセーシー

[特　徴]

基立ち、四股立ち等のすり足で体の移動により技を極め、その場での立ち方の変化により攻防の技の変化を表し、流し技など軽妙な技法と回し受けも特徴である。

NISESHI

[Characteristics]

In a characteristic Niseshi, a waza is executed by moving the body in a Suriashi from the Motodachi or Shikodachi standing position. Depending on the standing position, offensive and defensive wazas change. It is also characterized by quick and light techniques and Mawashiuke.

ニーセーシー

	直立 Stand	用意 Ready	1 挙動 Move	2 挙動 Move
手の動作 Hands	両手は開いて大腿前に軽く添える。 Open both hands and place them in front of the thighs, touching the thighs lightly.	両拳は握り、両大腿前に構える。 Grip both hands in front of the thighs.	右拳は引き手。左は猫手背屈し掌底（西向き、指上向き）。左体側より右体側へ胸前を横切って中段横払い。肘関節は約90°。 The right fist is in a Hikite. The left hand is in a Nekote-Haikutsu-Shotei (facing west, fingers -pointing up). Execute a Chudan-Yoko-Harai from the left side of the body to the right side crossing in front of the chest. The joint of the elbow is at about 90°.	左前腕の下を通して右中段突き。左猫手は、開手にして掌面下向き。 Execute a Right-Chudan-Tsuki under the left forearm. Maintain the Left-Nekote horizontally (the left palm facing down).
着眼点 Point to see	南 South	南 South	南 South	南 South
立ち方 Stance	結び立ち。 Musubidachi	閉足立ち。 Heisokudachi	左基立ち。 Left-Motodachi	左基立ち。 Left-Motodachi
北 North / 西 West / 東 East / 南 South			（白から黒へ動く。） (Move from White to Black.)	
足の動作 Feet	結び立ち。 Musubidachi	閉足立ち。 Heisokudachi	閉足立ちより右足を北に鋭く一歩引いて左足も少し引き、基立ち。 Starting with the Heisokudachi position, quickly pull the right foot one step towards the north. Pull the left foot slightly into the Motodachi position.	左足をすり足で南に進め、右足も同様に進める。 Move the left foot towards the south with a Suriashi. Similarly move the right foot.
留意点 Point			留意点 1 2 3 挙動 基立ちに引き込んでから、すり足で体を進め、左肘は関節付近に力点を置く。体は半身にならず正面に正対する。 In Movements 1, 2 and 3, pull the body into a Motodachi stance and move the body with a Suriashi to the south. Place the power point of the left elbow on the joint. The body faces to the front (not in Hanmi).	
動作の分解 Kumite in detail			①	

	3 挙動 Move	**4** 挙動　Move
	左手を拳にし、右前腕の下に入れながら甲面上向きで左前肘で突き放し、左前腕は胸前に平行に構える。右拳は引き手にする。 Grip the left hand, insert the fist under the right forearm. Push out (Tsukihanashi) the left elbow with the back of the hand facing up. Hold the left forearm in a parallel position in front of the chest. The right fist is in a Hikite.	両拳を引き手にし、左正拳（上）、右裏拳（下）の中段双手突き。両拳向かい合う。 Pull both fists (Hikite), execute a Chudan-Morote-Tsuki with the front part of the left fist (top) and the back part of the right fist (down). Both fists face each other.

	南 South	南 South	北 North	（北から見る） Seen from the north.
	❺ 右足立ち。 Stand on the right foot.	❻ 左基立ち。 Left-Motodachi.	❼ 右基立ち。 Right-Motodachi.	❼-A

| | 左踵は臀部を蹴るようにして、続いて南へすり足で出て、基立ち。

Kick the left heel as if kicking the hip, and move towards the south with a Suriashi and Motodachi. | | 左足を軸に右転し、北へ右基立ち。

Pivoting on the left foot, turn right. Execute a Right-Motodachi to the north. | |

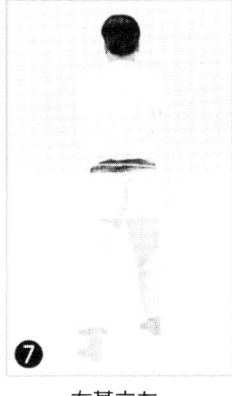

ニーセーシー

	5 挙 動 Move	**6** 挙 動 Move
手の動作 Hands	両拳を甲面外向きで胸前に垂直になるまで引き込む。 Pull both fists (back of the hands facing out) to the chest so that the arms are perpendicular to the body.	両腕尺骨側で双手中段に突き放す。両肘は曲げ、両甲面外向き。 On the elbow side of both arms, execute a Morote-Chudan (push out). Bend both elbows with the back of the hands facing out.
着眼点 Point to see	北 North / （北から見る）Seen from the north. ❽　❽-A 左足立ち。 Stand on the left foot.	北 North / （北から見る）Seen from the north. ❾　❾-A 右基立ち。 Right-Motodachi
立ち方 Stance		
北/西/東/南		
足の動作 Feet	右膝で下腹部に当てる。 Raise the right knee towards the lower abdomen.	右足を北にすり足でおろし、右基立ち。 Move the right foot down one step to the north with a Suriashi, and execute a Right-Motodachi.
留意点 Point	[備考] **5**、**6**挙動は連続して行う。 [Note] Execute Movements **5** and **6** continuously.	留意点**6**挙動　両拳は脇を締めて肩の高さに突き放す。両上腕は並行に立てる。 In Movement **6**, pull both elbows to the sides. Push the fists out. The fists are at shoulder level. Hold both forearms upward in a parallel position.
動作の分解 Kumite in detail	②	③

7 挙動 Move	**8** 挙動 Move
左上段受け。右拳引き手。 Left-Jodan-Uke. Right fist is in Hikite.	右肘前腕を甲面外向きで上段流し受け。左拳引き手。 Execute a Jodan-Nagashi-Uke with the right elbow and the forearm (the back of the hand facing outside). The left fist is in Hikite.

西 West	西 West	（西から見る） Seen from the west.
❿	⓫	⓫-A
左前屈立ち（順突き立ち）。 Left-Zenkutsudachi (Juntsukidachi)	左前屈立ち。 Left-Zenkutsudachi	

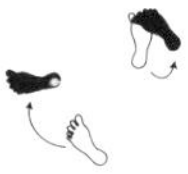

右足を軸にして左足を西へ出し。 Pivoting on the right foot, move the left foot towards the west.	そのまま。 Maintain the same position.

|留意点 **8** 挙動| 上半身を更に入り身に転じ、流し受けを行うと同時に肘打ちを行う。体軸を崩さず顔を背けない。

In Movement **8**, change the upper body position to Irimi. Execute a Nagashi-Uke and simultaneously execute a Hiji-Uchi. Maintain the body axis. Do not turn your face to the side.

④

151

ニーセーシー

9 挙 動　Move

手の動作 / Hands

右手で中段掛け受け。左手引き手はそのまま。

Execute a Chudan-Kake-Uke with the right hand. The left hand in Hikite remains the same.

右手を軽く伸ばし（⓭）。

Stretch the right arm lightly (⓭).

着眼点 / Point to see

東 / East　　　（北から見る）Seen from the north.

⓬　　　⓬－A

東 / East　　　（北から見る）Seen from the north.

⓭　　　⓭－A

立ち方 / Stance

四股立ち。Shikodachi

左足立ち。Standing on the left foot.

北 North / 西 West / 東 East / 南 South

足の動作 / Feet

左足を軸にして右転し、北向きに四股立ち。

Pivoting on the left foot, rotate the body to the right. Execute a Shikodachi facing north.

留意点 / Point

動作の分解 / Kumite in detail

⑤　　　⑥

152

10 挙 動　Move

右開手で掴み内捻りしながら右胸側に鋭く拳にして引きつける（⑭）。

Grab with the right hand. Turning it inward, grasp it and quickly pull the fist to the right side of the chest (⑭).

11 挙 動　Move

左拳で右斜め前方を中段突き。腕を緩めて胸前に鈎突きに構える。右拳引き手。

With the left fist, execute a Chudan-Tsuki diagonally to the front right. Loosen the arm and hold it in front of the chest for a Kagi-Tsuki. The right fist is in Hikite.

東
East

（北から見る）
Seen from the north.

東
East

（北から見る）
Seen from the north.

⑭
左足立ち。
Stand on the left foot.

⑭-A

⑮
四股立ち。
Shikodachi

⑮-A

左足を軸にし、右足膝を上げ（⑬）、下段蹴込み（⑭）。

Pivoting on the left foot, lift and move the right knee (⑬). Then execute a Gedan-Kerikomi (⑭).

右足を東に踏み出し、左足をすり足で寄せ、四股立ち。

Move the right foot one step towards the east. Pull the left foot (Suriashi), and Shikodachi.

[留意点⑩挙動] 蹴込みは体軸を垂直に保ち軸足の膝を伸ばしてはならない（右手の引きつけと蹴りは同時）。
［備考］ ⑨⑩⑪挙動は連続して行う。

In Movement ⑩, when executing a Keri-Komi, maintain a straight body axis. Do not stretch the knee of the pivoting leg. (Simultaneously pull the right hand and execute a Keri.)
[Note] Execute from Movement ⑨ to ⑪ continuously.

⑦

ニーセーシー

	12 挙 動 Move		**13** 挙 動 Move
手の動作 Hands	左手で中段掛け受け。右拳は引き手。 Execute a Chudan-Kake-Uke with the left hand. The right fist is in the Hikite position.	左手を軽く伸ばし（⑰）。 Extend the left arm lightly (⑰).	左開手で掴み内捻りしながら左胸側に鋭く拳にして引きつける（⑱）。 Grab with the left hand. Turning it inward, grasp it and quickly pull the fist to the left side of the chest (⑱).
着眼点 Point to see	西 West	西 West	西 West
立ち方 Stance	四股立ち。 Shikodachi	右足立ち。 Stand on the right foot.	右足立ち。 Stand on the right foot.
足の動作 Feet	四股立ち。 Shikodachi	右足を軸にし、左足膝を上げ（⑰）、下段蹴込み（⑱）。 Pivoting on the right foot, lift and move the left knee (⑰) and execute a Gedan-Kerikomi (⑱).	
留意点 Point			

北 North / 西 West / 東 East / 南 South

14 挙 動 Move

右拳で斜め前方を中段突き。腕を緩めて胸前に鉤突きに構える。左拳は引き手。

With the right fist, execute a Chudan-Tsuki diagonally to the front. Loosen the right arm and hold it in the Kagi-Tsuki position in front of the chest. The left fist is in the Hikite position.

両手猫手背屈し、左手指上向きで左腕側方に、右手指下向きで右腰側方に引いて構えながら。

Nekote-Haikutsu with both hands. Turning the left hand with fingers pointed up, pull the hand to the left side of the chest. Turning the right hand with fingers pointed down, pull the hand to the right side of the waist.

西
West

（北から見る）
Seen from the north.

北西
Northwest

（北から見る）
Seen from the north.

⑲

⑲-A

⑳

⑳-A

四股立ち。
Shikodachi

左足を西に踏み出し右足をすり足で寄せ四股立ち。

Move the left foot one step towards the west. Pull the right foot (Suriashi), and Shikodachi.

左足先を北西に向きを変えながら。

Turn the left foot, toes pointing towards the northwest.

［備考］ 12 13 14 挙動は連続して行う。

[Note] Execute from Movement 12 to 14 continuously.

ニーセーシー

	15 挙動 Move	**16 挙動 Move**
手の動作 Hands	右掌底で相手の左腸骨棘、左掌底で相手の右上胸部を双手突き。 Execute a Morote-Tsuki to the opponent's left iliac spine with the bottom of the right palm and to the opponent's right upper chest with the bottom of the left palm.	右手は背刀にし、掌面下向き右上肢を伸ばす。左拳は引き手。 Execute a Haito with the right hand; with the palm facing down, stretch the right upper arm. The left fist is in Hikite.
着眼点 Point to see	北西 Northwest ㉑　　（北から見る） 　　　Seen from the north. ㉑-A	南東 Southeast ㉒	南東 Southeast ㉓
立ち方 Stance	右前屈立ち。 Right-Zenkutsudachi		左前屈立ち。 Left-Zenkutsudachi
北 North / 西 West / 東 East / 南 South			
足の動作 Feet	北西方向に右足で踏み出し、前屈立ち。 Move the right foot one step towards the northwest, and Zenkutsudachi.	右足を軸に南東方向に左回りし、前屈立ち。 Pivoting on the right foot, turn left to the southeast and execute a Zenkutsudachi.	そのまま。 Maintain the same position.
留意点 Point			留意点16挙動 右背刀は、相手の目を横に切るか、コメカミを打つ。 In Movement 16, execute a Right Haito to cut the opponent's eye, horizontally, or hit the opponent's temple.
動作の分解 Kumite in detail		⑧	

156

17 挙 動 Move

右掌面に左背手を下から振り上げ、打ち当てる。

Execute a Left-Haite to the right palm by swinging the left hand up to hit the palm.

18 挙 動 Move

右手は平挟手を引き手にする。体を沈めながら左手は掬い手にし、前下方へ軽く伸ばす(㉕)。続いて、弧を描きながら左体側に掬い上げ、同時に右平挟手を下に突きおろす(㉖)。左手は拳にして引き手にする。

Execute a Hira-Hasamite with the right hand to a Hikite. Lowering the body, place the left hand in a Sukuite and stretch the hand lightly downwards in the front direction (㉕). Then, swing the left hand, scooping the hand up along the left side of the body. At the same time, execute a Right-Hira-Hasamite downward (㉖). Grasp (fist) the left hand and make a Hikite.

南東
Southeast

南東
Southeast

南東
Southeast

㉔

㉕

㉖

（北東から見る）
Seen from the northeast.

閉足立ち。
Heisokudachi

右T字立ち。
Right-T-ji-dachi

㉖-A

左足に右足を引き寄せ、閉足立ち。

Pull the right foot to the left foot, and execute a Heisoku-dachi.

左足を大きく北西に引く。

Pull the left foot wide to the northwest.

そのまま。

Maintain the same position.

[留意点 17挙動] 打ち当て音をたて、両手は伸ばしたまま。
[備考] 16と17挙動は連続して行う。

In Movement 17, make a hitting sound. Both hands remain extended.
[Note] Execute Movements 16 and 17 continuously.

[留意点 18 19挙動] 相手の蹴り足をかわすために、体を左に開く。平挟手は親指と揃えた他の指の間を開く。突きは腰を曲げないで真下に突きおろす。

In Movements 18 and 19, to dodge a Keri from an opponent, turn the body towards the left. Execute a Hira-Hasamite by stretching the thumb away from the other fingers. Execute a Tsuki straight down without bending the waist.

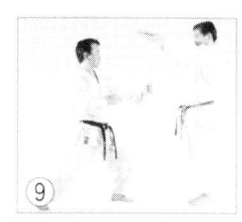

⑨

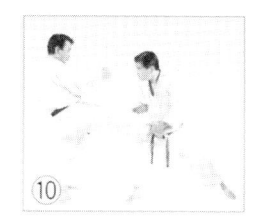

⑩

⑪

ニーセーシー

19 挙　動　Move

手の動作 / Hands

右手を素早く引き手にする（㉗）。	右拳裏突き、左正拳で双手下段突き（㉘）。
Execute a quick right Hikite (㉗).	Ura-Tsuki with a right fist. Morote-Gedan-Tsuki with a left fist (㉘).

着眼点 / Point to see

南東	南東下方	（北から見る）
Southeast	Lower southeast.	Seen from the north.
㉗	㉘	㉘-A

立ち方 / Stance

右Ｔ字立ち。	右Ｔ字立ち。	
Right-T-ji-dachi.	Right-T-ji-dachi	

北 North / 西 West — 東 East / 南 South

足の動作 / Feet

そのまま。	そのまま。
Maintain the same position.	Maintain the same position.

留意点 / Point

留意点 19挙動　両拳掌面は向かい合う。左拳が上。	［備考］ 18と19挙動は連続して行う。
In Movement 19, the palms of both fists face each other. The left fist is on top.	[Note] Execute Movements 18 and 19 continuously.

158

20 挙 動 Move	21 挙 動 Move
左は中段掛け受け。右拳は引き手。	右手は甲面前向き上段流し受け。左手は引き手。
Execute a Chudan-Kake-Uke with the left hand. The right fist is in Hikite.	Execute a Jodan-Nagashi-Uke with the right hand (the back of the hand facing front). The left hand is in Hikite.

北西
Northwest

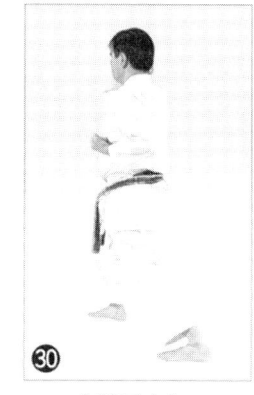

（北から見る）
Seen from the north.

㉙

左真半身猫足立ち。
Left-Mahanmi-Nekoashidachi

㉙－A

北西
Northwest

（北から見る）
Seen from the north.

㉚

右前屈立ち。
Right-Zenkutsudachi

㉚－A

体を起こし、右足を軸にして北西に左真半身猫足立ち。

Raise the body, pivoting on the right foot, and execute a Left-Mahanmi-Nekoashidachi towards the northwest.

右足を北西に進め、前屈立ち。

Move the right foot towards the northwest, and Zenkutsudachi.

ニーセーシー

	22 挙動 Move	**23 挙動 Move**	**24 挙動 Move**	
手の動作 Hands	右下段払い。左拳は引き手。 Execute a Right-Gedan-Harai. The left fist is in Hikite.	その場で左逆突き。 Execute a Left-Gyaku-Tsuki at the position.	左中段掛け受け。右拳は引き手。 Execute a Left-Chudan-Kake-Uke. The right fist is in Hikite.	
着眼点 Point to see	北西 Northwest	北西 Northwest	南 South	南 South
	㉛	㉜	㉝	㉞
立ち方 Stance	四股立ち。 Shikodachi	右縦セイシャン立ち。 Right-Tate-Seishandachi	左真半身猫足立ち。 Left-Mahanmi-Nekoashidachi	
足の動作 Feet	その場で四股立ち。 Shikodachi at the position.	右足を引きながら（北西）右縦セイシャン立ち。 Pulling the right foot (northwest), execute a Tate-Seishandachi.	右足を軸にして南方向に左真半身猫足立ち。 Pivoting on the right foot, execute a Left-Mahanmi-Nekoashidachi towards the south.	左足を軸に右足を左転して南方向に。 Pivoting on the left foot, rotate the right foot to the left, facing south.

方位: 北 North / 西 West / 東 East / 南 South

留意点 ㉑㉒㉓挙動 前屈立ち、四股立ち、縦セイシャン立ちの変化を正確にリズミカルに使い分ける。
[備考] ㉑、㉒、㉓挙動は連続して行う。

In Movements ㉑, ㉒ and ㉓, change the standing positions (Zenkutsudachi, Shikodachi, Tate-Seishandachi) precisely and rhythmically.
[Note] Execute Movements from ㉑ to ㉓ continuously.

25 挙 動 Move	26 挙 動 Move
左手刀を胸前に平手に構え、右肘打ちを左手掌に当てる（甲前向き）。	右拳槌で右斜め前下方に下腹部打ち。左前腕上向きに胸前に構える。
Hold the Left-Shuto with Hirate in front of the chest. Place the Right-Hiji-Uchi on the left palm. (The back of the hand facing front.)	Execute a Kafukubu-Uchi in the lower right direction with a right Kentsui. Hold the left forearm upward in front of the chest.

東
East

（南東から見る）
Seen from the southeast.

東
East

（南東から見る）
Seen from the southeast.

㉟ 四股立ち。
Shikodachi

㉟-A

㊱ 四股立ち。
Shikodachi

㊱-A

東方向に四股立ち。
Shikodachi facing east.

そのまま。
Maintain the same position.

［備考］ 25、26挙動は連続して行う。

[Note] Execute Movements 25 and 26 continuously.

ニーセーシー

	27 挙動 Move	28 挙動 Move	29 挙動 Move	30 挙動 Move
手の動作 Hands	北東に左中段掛け受け。右拳は引き手。 Execute a Left-Chudan-Kake-Uke towards the northeast. The right fist is in Hikite.	甲面前向き右上段流し受け。左拳は引き手。 Execute a Right-Jodan-Nagashi-Uke with the back of the right hand facing front. The left fist is in Hikite.	右下段払い。左拳は引き手。 Execute a Right-Gedan-Harai. The left fist is in Hikite.	その場で左中段逆突き。 Execute a Left-Chudan-Gyaku-Tsuki at the position.
着眼点 Point to see	北東 Northeast	北東 Northeast	北東 Northeast	北東 Northeast
	③⑦	③⑧	③⑨	④⓪
立ち方 Stance	左真半身猫足立ち。 Left-Mahanmi-Nekoashidachi	右前屈立ち。 Right-Zenkutsudachi	四股立ち。 Shikodachi	右縦セイシャン立ち。 Right-Tate-Seishandachi
足の動作 Feet	右足を軸に左足を北東方向に左真半身猫足立ち。 Pivoting on the right foot, move the left foot northeast, and stand in a Left-Mahanmi-Nekoashidachi.	左足を軸に右足を北東方向に進め、右前屈立ち。 Pivoting on the left foot, move the right foot towards the northeast, and execute a Right-Zenkutsudachi.	その場で四股立ち。北西向き。 Shikodachi at the position. Face to the northwest.	足はその場で右縦セイシャン立ち。 Both feet are Right-Tate-Seishandachi at the position.
留意点 Point		[備考] 28 29 30 挙動は連続して行う。 [Note] Execute from Movement 28 to 30 continuously.		
動作の分解 Kumite in detail				

31 挙動 Move

両拳を引き手にしながら（㊷）。

Having both hands in Hikite (㊷).

右正拳。左は裏拳で中段双手突き（㊸）。

Hold the right hand in Seiken. Execute a Chudan-Morote-Tsuki with Uraken (㊸).

北東 Northeast	南 South	南 South	南 South
㊶	㊷	㊸	㊹
	左横セイシャン立ち。Left-Yoko-Seishandachi	左横セイシャン立ち。Left-Yoko-Seishandachi	

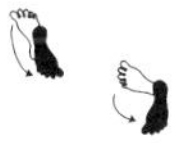

左足を軸に右足を左転して、南方向に左横セイシャン立ち。

Pivoting on the left foot, rotate the right foot to the left, and execute a Left-Yoko-Seishandachi towards the south.

そのまま。

Maintain the same position.

そのまま。

Maintain the same position.

⑫

163

ニーセーシー

	32 挙動 Move	止め Stop	直立 Stand
手の動作 Hands	両手開手にしながら右を前腸骨に引き（指先は下向き）、左は左胸に引き（指先は上向き）、掌面は南（㊺）。 Opening both hands, pull the right hand to the front iliac bone (fingers are facing down). Pull the left hand to the left side of the chest (fingers are facing up). The palm is facing south (㊺).	続いて、右手掌は下段、左は手刀にして上胸部にゆっくり押し出す（正中線、㊻）。 Slowly push out the right palm into a Gedan and slowly push out the left hand (Shuto) to the upper chest (Seichusen, ㊻).	大腿前面に拳を下げる。 Lower the fists so they are in front of the thighs.	両手は開いて大腿前に軽く添える。 Open both hands and place them in front of the thighs, touching the thighs lightly.
着眼点 Point to see	南 South ㊺	南 South ㊻	南 South ㊼	南 South ㊽
立ち方 Stance	閉足立ち。 Heisokudachi	閉足立ち。 Heisokudachi	閉足立ち。 Heisokudachi	結び立ち。 Musubidachi
北 North 西 West — 東 East 南 South				
足の動作 Feet	右足に左足を引き寄せ、閉足立ち。 Pull the left foot to the right foot, and execute a Heisokudachi.	閉足立ち。 Heisokudachi	閉足立ち。 Heisokudachi	結び立ち。 Musubidachi

留意点 Point

留意点 31 32 挙動 回し受けは両手開手にし、右手を背屈し小手返しをしながら掛け受けにして、ゆっくり体側に引き込み両手を正面にゆっくり押し出す。

In Movements 31 and 32, execute a Mawashi-Uke with the open palms. Holding the right hand in a Haikutsu, execute a Kote-Kaeshi moving into the Kake-Uke position. Slowly pull the right hand to the body and slowly push both hands out to the front.

動作の分解
Kumite in detail

⑬ ⑭ ⑮

クーシャンクー

[特　徴]

　この形は首里系で観空大、公相君(コーソークン)等の名称で親しまれている形である。和道流のこの形は真半身猫足立ち手刀受けが特徴といえる。形としては挙動数の多い方に属し、基本技が多く含まれ、特に上段への攻撃に対し体を低くし反撃に転ずるなど軽快で敏捷な形である。

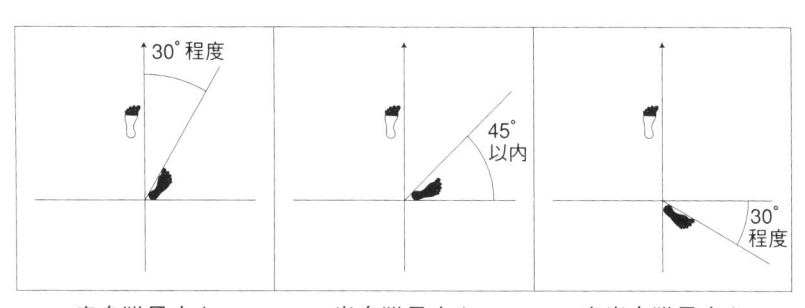

真身猫足立ち Mami-Nekoashidachi	半身猫足立ち Hanmi-Nekoashidachi	真半身猫足立ち Mahanmi-Nekoashidachi
30°程度	45°以内	30°程度

重心は何れも軸足に2/3、前足に1/3の配分である。
Two-thirds (2/3) of the center of gravity should be on the pivoting foot and one-third on the front foot.

KUSHANKU

[Characteristics]

The Kata, which comes under Shuri-Kei, is popularly known under the names of Kanku-Dai or Kosokun.
The most distinctive characteristic involved in this Wado-Ryu-derived kata, are said to be Mahanmi-Nekoachidachi Shuto-Uke. As a Kata, it can be categorized within the kata with various movements and the many of which included are used as the basics. Particularly those skills that take quick and fast movements are used in counter-attacks from the low positions.

クーシャンクー

	直 立 Stand	用 意 Ready		
手の動作 Hands	両手は開いて大腿前に軽く添える。 Open both hands and place them in front of the thighs, touching the thighs lightly.	右手甲面と左手掌を重ね、体の直前に下げて構える。 Open both hands, place the left palm on the back of the right hand. Hold them in front of the body.		
着眼点 Point to see	南 South	南 South	南 South	南 South
	❶	❷	❸	❹
立ち方 Stance	結び立ち。 Musubidachi	八字立ち。 Hachijidachi	八字立ち。 Hachijidachi	八字立ち。 Hachijidachi
北 North 西 West ─┼─ 東 East 南 South		（白から黒へ動く。） (Move from White to Black.)		
足の動作 Feet	結び立ち。 Musubidachi	結び立ちから足を左、右と開き、八字立ちとなる（両踵の間隔は2足長、肩幅より広く）。 From the Musubidachi position, spread both legs left and right to a Hachijidachi (the width between the heels should be slightly wider than the shoulder width).	❷と同じく。 Same as the Ready position ❷.	
留意点 Point	留意点 クーシャンクーの「八字立ち」は総じてセイシャン、チントウの形の八字立ちより広い足幅になっている。 The width of a Hachijidachi in a Kushanku is wider than a Hachijidachi in Seishan's and Chinto's form.			

166

1 挙動 Move	**2** 挙動 Move		**3** 挙動 Move
両手を重ねたまま前から静かに挙上(やや前方)し(❸)、両手を手刀にして左右に円を描き(❹)、元の位置に薬指が触れる程度に構える(❺)。	左背手で上段払い受け。右手は甲面下向き胸前に構える。		右背手で上段払い受け。左手は甲面下向き胸前に構える。
While keeping both hands together, quietly raise them above the head (slightly forward) (❸). Lower both hands (in Shuto) to the side, inscribing a circle (❹). Return the hands to the Ready position but with the palms facing to the front and the third fingers touching (❺).	Execute a Jodan-Harai-Uke with the left hand (Left-Haite). Hold the right hand in front of the chest (the back of the hand is facing down).		Execute a Jodan-Harai-Uke with the right hand (Right-Haite). Hold the left hand in front of the chest (the back of the hand is facing down).

南	東	西	西
South	East	West	West

❺ 八字立ち。
Hachijidachi

❻ 左真半身猫足立ち。
Left-Mahanmi-Nekoashidachi

❼

❽ 右真半身猫足立ち。
Right-Mahanmi-Nekoashidachi

	八字立ちから左足を東へ出す。		左足を元に戻し、右足を西へ出す。
	From Hachijidachi, move the left foot towards the east.		Return the left foot to the original position and move the right foot towards the west.

クーシャンクー

	4 挙動 Move	**5 挙動 Move**	**6 挙動 Move**	
手の動作 Hands	両手を拳にし、右拳は引き手。左拳は甲面上向き胸前で構える（左拳は道着に触れる程度）。 Grasp both hands. The right fist is in Hikite. Hold the left fist (the back of the hand facing up) in front of the chest. Hold the left fist as it lightly touches the dogi.	左腕で前中段払い。 Execute a Mae-Chudan-Harai with the left arm.	続いて右拳中段突き。 Continuously execute a Chudan-Tsuki with the right fist.	右拳は足の移動と共に左下方におろし。 As the feet move, lower the right fist to the lower left side.
着眼点 Point to see	南 South ❾	南 South ❿	南 South ⓫	南 South ⓬
立ち方 Stance	八字立ち。 Hachijidachi	八字立ち。 Hachijidachi	八字立ち。 Hachijidachi	
足の動作 Feet	右足を元に戻し、八字立ちとなる。 Return the right foot to the original position, and stand in the Hachijidachi position.	そのまま。 Maintain the same position.	そのまま。 Maintain the same position.	左足を東へ広く移す（四股立ち程度）。 Shift the left foot in a wide stance towards east (equivalent to Shikodachi).
留意点 Point			［備考］ 5、6挙動は連続して行う。 [Note] Execute Movements 5 and 6 continuously.	

7 挙動 Move	8 挙 動 Move		9 挙動 Move
体の捻りに合わせて右上段外受け。	左中段突き。右拳は引き手。	左拳は足の移動と共に右下方におろし。	体の捻りに合わせて左上段外受け。
Twisting the body, execute a Right-Jodan-Soto-Uke.	Execute a Left-Chudan-Tsuki. The right fist is in Hikite.	As the feet move, lower the left fist to the lower right side.	Twisting the body, execute a Left-Jodan-Soto-Uke.

南 South	南 South	南 South	南 South
⑬	⑭	⑮	⑯
横セイシャン立ちの応用。	八字立ち。	⑫の逆。	⑬の逆。
Apply a Yoko-Seishandachi.	Hachijidachi	Reverse of ⑫	Reverse of ⑬

	左足を引き、八字立ちとなる。	右足を西へ広く移す（四股立ち程度）。	
	Pull the left foot to a Hachiji-dachi.	Step wide to the west (width of Shikodachi) with the right foot.	

[留意点 7 8 挙動] 足を左へ運ぶと同時に肘の力を抜き、体の捻りで上段外受けを行い、その反動を利用して中段突きに極める。

In Movements 7 and 8, simultaneously move the left foot to the left, relax the elbow, execute a Jodan-Soto-Uke by twisting the body. Using the reflex, execute a Chudan-Tsuki.

［備考］ 7 〜 8 挙動は連続して行う。

[Note] Execute Movements 7 and 8 continuously.

クーシャンクー

🔟 挙 動　Move

手の動作 / Hands

北の上段外受け（蹴りと受けは同時）。

Execute a North-Jodan-Soto-Uke.
(Execute a Keri and a Uke simultaneously.)

着眼点 / Point to see

南 South	北 North	（北から見る）Seen from the north.	南 South
⑰	⑱	⑱-A	⑲

立ち方 / Stance

左足立ち。
Stand on the left foot.

北 North / 西 West / 東 East / 南 South

足の動作 / Feet

左足を右足近くへ移し。
Move the left foot near the right foot.

右足は北へ横蹴り。
Execute a Yoko-Keri to the north with the right foot.

留意点 / Point

170

11 挙 動 Move	**12** 挙 動 Move	**13** 挙 動 Move
左上段手刀受け。右手刀は胸前に構える。	右上段手刀受け。左手刀は胸前に構える。	左上段手刀受け。右手刀は胸前に構える。
Execute a Left-Jodan-Shuto-Uke. Hold the right Shuto in front of the chest.	Execute a Right-Jodan-Shuto-Uke. Hold the left Shuto in front of the chest.	Execute a Left-Jodan-Shuto-Uke. Hold the right Shuto in front of the chest.

南
South

⑳

左真半身猫足立ち。
Left-Mahanmi-Nekoashidachi

南
South

㉑

南
South

㉒

右真半身猫足立ち。
Right-Mahanmi-Nekoashidachi

南
South

㉓

左真半身猫足立ち。
Left-Mahanmi-Nekoashidachi

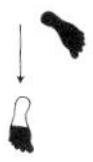

右足を左足脇に添えておろし、左足を南へ出す。

Place the right foot at the side of the left foot. Move the left foot towards the south.

右足を南へ出す。

Move the right foot towards the south.

左足を南へ出す。

Move the left foot towards the south.

171

クーシャンクー

	14 挙動 Move	**15** 挙動 Move
手の動作 Hands	右中段貫手突き。 Execute a Right-Chudan-Nukite-Tsuki.	右手掌で中段払い。左手は手刀とし、額前に構える。 Execute a Chudan-Harai with a right palm. The left hand is in Shuto; hold it in front of the forehead.
着眼点 Point to see	南 South	北 North / 北 North / （北から見る）Seen from the north.
立ち方 Stance	㉔ 右前屈立ち(順突き立ち)。 Right-Zenkutsudachi (Jun-Tsukidachi)	㉕ / ㉖ 横セイシャン立ちの応用。 Apply a Yoko-Seishandachi. / ㉖－A
足の動作 Feet	右足を南へ出す。 Move the right foot towards the south.	右足を軸にして北へ左回りする。 Pivoting on the right foot, turn left facing north.
留意点 Point		
動作の分解 Kumite in detail		①

16 挙 動 Move	17 挙 動 Move	18 挙 動 Move
そのまま。 Maintain the same position.	左右を拳として右拳上段、左拳下段に構える。 Grasp both hands. Hold the right fist up (Jodan) and hold the left fist down (Gedan).	左拳掌面上向、胸前に構える。右手は伸ばして左手の下に交差させる。 Hold the left fist (the palm side facing up) in front of the chest. Extend the right arm so it crosses under the left hand.

北
North

（北から見る）
Seen from the north.

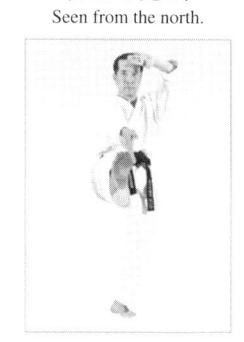

南
South

南
South

㉗ 左足立ち。
Stand on the left foot.

㉗-A

㉘ 右爪先立ち。
Right-Tsumasakidachi

㉙ 右爪先立ち。
Right-Tsumasakidachi

| 北へ右中段蹴り。

Execute a Right-Chudan-Keri towards the north. | 蹴り足を引き、やや南西に爪先立ちでおろす。

Retract the kicked leg and step forward towards the southwest and stand on the toes. | そのまま。

Maintain the same position. |

留意点 16 17 18 19 挙動　蹴り足を引くと同時に、膝を内屈しながら体を低くして両拳を構える。この構えは、攻守どちらにも対応できるようにすること。屈した右膝は踵を臀部に接してはならない。連続動作の中で下段突きを鋭く極める。

In Movements 16, 17, 18 and 19, pull the right leg (the leg used to kick) back towards the body, at the same time, lower the body and hold both fists while bending the knee inward. In this position, the player shall be ready for both offensive and defensive actions. The right hip should not touch the back of the right heel (right knee is bent). In continuous movements, execute a Gedan-Tsuki quickly.

②  ③  ④

クーシャンクー

	19 挙 動 Move	20 挙 動 Move		21 挙 動 Move
手の動作 Hands	左拳下段突き。右拳は引き手。 Execute a Gedan-Tsuki with the left fist. The right fist is in Hikite.	右手掌で中段払い。左手は手刀とし、額前に構える。 Execute a Chudan-Harai with a right palm. The left hand is in a Shuto; hold it in front of the forehead.		そのまま。 Maintain the same position.
着眼点 Point to see	南 South ㉚	南 South ㉛	南 South ㉜	南 South ㉝
立ち方 Stance	八字立ち。 Hachijidachi		横セイシャン立ちの応用。 Apply a Yoko-Seishandachi.	左足立ち。 Stand on the left foot.
北 North 西 West ― 東 East 南 South				
足の動作 Feet	左足を北へ引き、立ち上がり八字立ちとなる。 Pull the left foot towards the north. When standing up, make a Hachijidachi.	右足を軸にして南へ左回りする。 Pivoting on the right foot, turn left towards the south.		南へ右中段蹴り。 Execute a Right-Chudan-Keri towards the south.
留意点 Point	[備考] 15〜19挙動は連続で行う。 [Note] Execute from Movement 15 to 19 continuously.			
動作の分解 Kumite in detail	⑤			

22 挙動 Move	23 挙動 Move	24 挙動 Move
左右を拳として右拳上段、左拳下段に構る。 Grasp both hands. Hold the right fist up (Jodan) and hold the left fist down (Gedan).	左拳掌面上向、胸前に構える。右手は伸ばして左手の下に交差させる。 Hold the left fist (the palm side facing up) in front of the chest. Extend the right arm so it crosses under the left hand.	左拳下段突き。右拳は引き手。 Execute a Gedan-Tsuki with the left fist. The right fist is in Hikite.
北 North	北 North	北 North
 ㉞	 ㉟	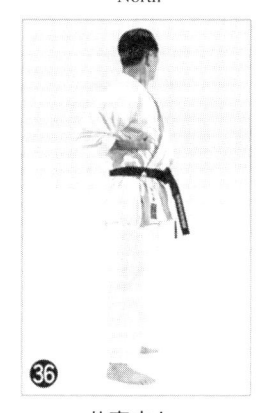 ㊱
右爪先立ち。 Right-Tsumasakidachi	右爪先立ち。 Right-Tsumasakidachi	八字立ち。 Hachijidachi
蹴り足を引き、やや北東に爪先立ちでおろす。 Retract the kicked leg and step forward towards the northeast and stand on the toes.	そのまま。 Maintain the same position.	左足を南へ引き、立ち上がり八字立ちとなる。 Pull the left foot towards the south. When standing up, make a Hachijidachi.

［備考］⑳〜㉔挙動は連続で行う。

[Note] Execute from Movement ⑳ to ㉔ continuously.

クーシャンクー

	25 挙動 Move	26 挙動 Move	27 挙動 Move
手の動作 Hands	右拳は引き手のまま、左拳は胸前水平に構える（道着に軽く触れる程度）。 The right fist remains in Hikite. Hold the left fist horizontally so it is at the front chest level. (Hold the left fist as it lightly touches the dogi.)	右拳は引き手。左拳は西へ中段払い（払いと蹴りは同時）。 The right fist is in Hikite. Execute a Chudan-Harai to the west with the left fist. (Execute a Harai and a Keri simultaneously.)	左足の着地と同時に右肘打ちをする。 At the moment that the left foot touches the floor, execute a Right-Hiji-Uchi.
着眼点 Point to see	西 West / （北から見る）Seen from the north.	西 West	西 West
立ち方 Stance	㉟ 閉足立ち。 Heisokudachi / ㉟-A	㊳ 右足立ち。 Stand on the right foot.	㊴ 左逆突き立ち。 Left-Gyaku-Tsukidachi
足の動作 Feet	左足を引きつつ、体を北へ向け、閉足で立つ。 Pulling the left foot, turn the body to the north and stand in a Heisokudachi position.	右足を軸にして左足で西へ横蹴りをする。 Pivoting on the right foot, with the left foot execute a Yoko-Keri to the west.	左足を西へおろす。 Move the left foot down towards the west.
留意点 Point		[備考] 26、27挙動は連続で行う。 留意点26挙動 横蹴りは膝頭を上げて蹴る。その時、引き手側の肩が蹴る方向に回ったり上半身が左右に傾斜しないこと。 [Note] Execute Movements 26 and 27 continuously. In Movement 26, execute a Yoko-Keri by raising the patella. Do not pull the shoulder (Hikite side) in the kicking direction or do not move the upper body to the right or left.	

28 挙動 Move	29 挙動 Move	30 挙 動 Move
左拳は引き手のまま、右拳は胸前水平に構える（道着に軽く触れる程度）。	左拳は引き手。右拳は東へ中段払い（払いと蹴りは同時）。	右足の着地と同時に左肘打ちをする。
The left fist remains in Hikite. Hold the right fist horizontally so it is at the front chest level. (Hold the right fist as it lightly touches the dogi.)	The left fist is in Hikite. Execute a Chudan-Harai to the east with the right fist. (Execute a Harai and a Keri simultaneously.)	At the moment that the right foot touches the floor, execute a Left-Hiji-Uchi.

東
East

東
East

東
East

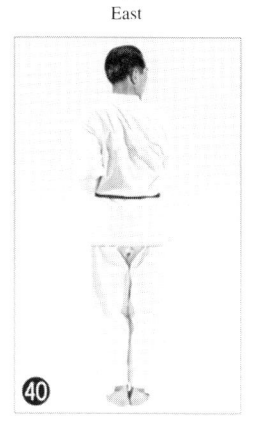

（東から見る）
Seen from the east.

�
閉足立ち。
Heisokudachi

㊶
左足立ち。
Stand on the left foot.

㊷
右逆突き立ち。
Right-Gyaku-Tsukidachi

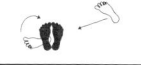

㊷－A

右足を左足に引きつけて閉足立ちとする。	左足を軸にして右足で東へ横蹴りする。	右足を東へおろす。
Pull the right foot to the left foot and stand in the Heisokudachi position.	Pivoting on the left foot, with the right foot execute a Yoko-Keri to the east.	Move the right foot down towards the east.

［備考］29、30挙動は連続で行う。

[Note] Execute Movements 29 and 30 continuously.

177

クーシャンクー

		31 挙動 Move	32 挙動 Move	33 挙動 Move
手の動作 Hands		左上段手刀受け。右手刀は胸前に構える。 Execute a Left-Jodan-Shuto-Uke. Hold the right Shuto in front of the chest.	右上段手刀受け。左手刀は胸前に構える。 Execute a Right-Jodan-Shuto-Uke. Hold the left Shuto in front of the chest.	右上段手刀受け。左手刀は胸前に構える。 Execute a Right-Jodan-Shuto-Uke. Hold the left Shuto in front of the chest.
着眼点 Point to see		西 West ㊸	西 West ㊹	北西 Northwest ㊺	東 East ㊻
立ち方 Stance			左真半身猫足立ち。 Left-Mahanmi-Nekoashidachi	右真半身猫足立ち。 Right-Mahanmi-Nekoashidachi	右真半身猫足立ち。 Right-Mahanmi-Nekoashidachi
北 North 西 West — 東 East 南 South					
足の動作 Feet		逆突き立ちから、右足を軸にして左方向（東から西）へ体を開き、左真半身猫足立ちとなる。 From the Gyaku-Tsukidachi, pivoting on the right foot, move the body to the left (from east to west) and stand in the Left-Mahanmi-Nekoashidachi position.		左足を軸にして北西へ右真半身猫足立ちとなる。 Pivoting on the left foot, stand in the Right-Mahanmi-Nekoashidachi position towards the northwest.	左足を軸にして東へ右回りし、右真半身猫足立ちとなる。 Pivoting on the left foot, turn to the east (to the right), and stand in the Right-Mahanmi-Nekoashidachi position.
留意点 Point					
動作の分解 Kumite in detail					

34 挙動 Move

左上段手刀受け。右手刀は胸前に構える。

Execute a Left-Jodan-Shuto-Uke. Hold the right Shuto in front of the chest.

35 挙動 Move

右手拳で中段払い。左手は手刀とし、額前に構える。

Execute a Chudan-Harai with a right fist. The left hand is in Shuto; hold it in front of the forehead.

36 挙動 Move

北東 / Northeast

北 / North

北 / North

（北西から見る）
Seen from the Northwest.

㊼ 左真半身猫足立ち。
Left-Mahanmi-Nekoashidachi

㊽ 横セイシャン立ちの応用。
Apply a Yoko-Seishandachi

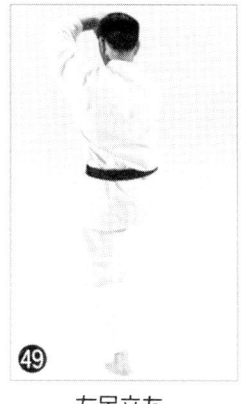

㊾ 左足立ち。
Stand on the left foot

㊾-A

右足を軸にして左足を北東へ出す。

Pivoting on the right foot, move the left foot toward the northeast.

右足を軸にして左足を西へ移動。

Pivoting on the right foot, move the left foot towards the west.

左足を軸にして右足で中段前蹴りをする（㊾）。

Pivoting on the left foot, execute a Chudan-Mae-Keri with the right foot (㊾).

留意点 35 36 37 挙動 蹴った体を正面に直しながら飛び込む時、左拳は体の中心より中段落し受けをしながら、右拳は内側を通って上段裏打ちに極める。爪先立ちは重心を等分に立つ。

In Movements 35, 36 and 37, after jumping in and executing a Keri, raise the body to an upward position facing front. At the same time, execute a Chudan-Otoshi-Uke with the left fist from the center of the body. Push the right fist through and under the left arm and execute a Jodan-Ura-Uchi. In Tsumasakidachi, maintain the center of gravity in the center of the body.

⑥

179

クーシャンクー

	37 挙 動 Move	**38** 挙 動 Move
手の動作 Hands	蹴りの後、体を北へ向けながら飛び込み右裏拳上段打ち。左手刀は中段を落し受けとし、拳にして引き手とする。 After the kick (Keri), turn the body to the north and jump (Tobikomi), execute a Right-Uraken-Jodan-Uchi. Execute a Otoshi-Uke in Chudan with the left Shuto and make a fist and execute a Hikite.	左引き手はそのまま、右上段外受けをする。 Hold the left Hikite as is and execute a Right-Jodan-Soto-Uke.
着眼点 Point to see	北 North　　　（北から見る） 　　　　　　　Seen from the north. ㊾	北 North　　　（北から見る） 　　　　　　　Seen from the north. ㊿
立ち方 Stance	左爪先立ち。 Left-Tsumasakidachi　　㊾−A	右前屈立ち。 Right-Zenkutsudachi　　㊿−A
北 North 西 West ─ 東 East 南 South		
足の動作 Feet	左足は右踵に添え、爪先立ち。 Place the left foot at the right heel and stand on the toes (Tsumasakidachi).	爪先立ちから左足を南方向へ素早く引き、下がりながら前屈立ちとなる。 From the Tsumasakidachi position, quickly pull the left foot towards the south, move back and stand in the Zenkutsudachi position.
留意点 Point		
動作の分解 Kumite in detail	⑦	

180

39 挙　動　Move	**40** 挙　動　Move
左中段突き。	右中段突き。
Execute a Left-Chudan-Tsuki.	Execute a Right-Chudan-Tsuki.

北
North

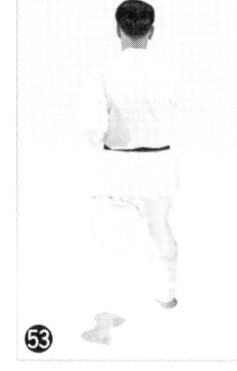

（北から見る）
Seen from the north.

北
North

（北から見る）
Seen from the north.

52

右前屈立ち。
Right-Zenkutsudachi

52-A

53

右前屈立ち。
Right-Zenkutsudachi

53-A

そのまま。
Maintain the same position.

そのまま。
Maintain the same position.

［備考］ **39**～**40**挙動は連続して行う。

[Note] Execute Movements **39** and **40** continuously.

クーシャンクー

	41 挙動 Move		**42** 挙動 Move
手の動作 Hands		左手掌で右大腿内側を打ち、膝の少し上に手刀にして構え、右拳槌を添える（両手と膝の動きは同時）。 Hit the inner right thigh with the left palm. Hold a Shuto just above the knee and place a right Kentsui on the left hand. (Simultaneously move both hands and the right knee.)	両手は肩幅程度に開き、指を軽く床に着ける。 Open both arms to shoulder width. Fingers should touch the floor lightly.
着眼点 Point to see	南 South	南 South　（南東から見る） Seen from the southeast.	南下方 South, down
立ち方 Stance	㊴	㊵ 左足立ち。 Stand on the left foot.　㊵-A	㊶ 両足爪先立ち。 Stand on the toes (Ryo-Ashi-Tsumasakidachi)
足の動作 Feet		左足を軸にして左回りで南へ向く。右足で前蹴りする如く膝を上げる。 Pivoting on the left foot, turn to the south (to the left). Raise the right knee as if to execute a kick (Mae-Keri).	南方向へ順突きの歩幅で両足を爪先立ちとなる。 Stand on the toes (Tsumasaki dachi) facing south. The width between the feet should be the same as for a Jun-Tsuki.
留意点 Point	留意点 40 41 42 挙動　南に振り向いた時、目線を下に向けたりフェイントの両手を高く上げて構えてはならない。軸足を動かさないで体を真っ直ぐに倒し両爪立ちで低く構える。右膝頭を体側にやや外し両手指先は床に軽く触れる。目線は2～3m先を見る。 In Movements 40, 41 and 42, when turning to the south, do not look down and do not raise both hands too high in a feint. While maintaining the body on the pivoted foot, bend into a low position and hold in a Ryotsumasakidachi. Move the right knee-top a little outward and lightly touch the floor with the fingertips of both hands. Look 2 or 3 meters ahead.		
動作の分解 Kumite in detail	⑧	⑨	⑩

43 挙 動　Move

左上段手刀受け。右手刀は胸前に構える。

Execute a Left-Jodan-Shuto-Uke. Hold a right Shuto in front of the chest.

北
North

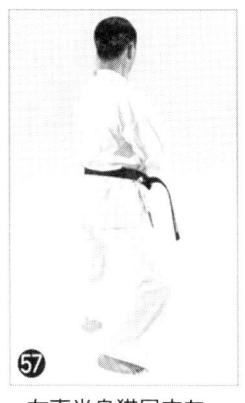

（北から見る）
Seen from the north.

❺❼

❺❼-A

左真半身猫足立ち。
Left-Mahanmi-Nekoashidachi

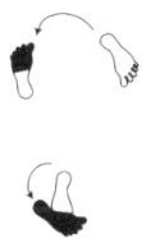

即立ち上がり、左足を少し引き、北へ左真半身猫足立ちとなる。

Quickly stand up, pull the left foot a little and stand in the Left-Mahanmi-Nekoashidachi position facing north.

［備考］ ㊶〜㊸挙動は連続して行う。

[Note] Execute from Movement ㊶ to ㊸ continuously.

44 挙 動　Move

右上段手刀受け。左手刀は胸前に構える。

Execute a Right-Jodan-Shuto-Uke. Hold a left Shuto in front of the chest.

北
North

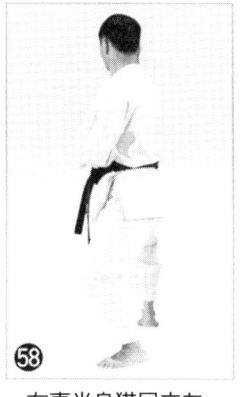

（北から見る）
Seen from the north.

❺❽

❺❽-A

右真半身猫足立ち。
Right-Mahanmi-Nekoashidachi

右足を一歩北へ出し、右真半身猫足立ちとなる。

Move the right foot one step towards the north, and stand in the Right-Mahanmi-Nekoashidachi position.

クーシャンクー

		45 挙動 Move	**46** 挙動 Move	
手の動作 Hands		左上段外受け。右手は引き手。 Execute a Left-Jodan-Soto-Uke. The right fist is in the Hikite position.	右拳中段突き。左拳は引き手。 Execute a Chudan-Tsuki with the right fist. The left fist is in the Hikite position.	
着眼点 Point to see	東 East	東 East	東 East	西 West
立ち方 Stance		左真身猫足立ち。 Left-Mami-Nekoashidachi	左真身猫足立ち。 Left-Mami-Nekoashidachi	
北 North 西 West — 東 East 南 South				
足の動作 Feet		右足を軸にして左回りで東へ向き、左真身猫足立ちとなる(体の向きは東)。 Pivoting on the right foot, turn counterclockwise and face the east, and Left-Mami-Nekoashidachi. (The body faces to east.)	そのまま。 Maintain the same position.	

留意点 **44 45 46 挙動** 右真半身猫足立ちより左真身猫足立ちになる時、右足に重心を移しながら上半身の軸を真っ直ぐ保ち回転する。その時、左拳は力を抜いて腰の回転に合わせて上段外受けをする。

In Movements **44**, **45** and **46**, when the standing position changes from a Right-Mahanmi-Nekoashidachi to a Left-Mami-Nekoashidachi moving the center of gravity to the right foot, rotate the upper body while maintaining a straight body axis. At the same time, relax the left fist and execute a Jodan-Soto-Uke when rotating the waist.

47 挙動 Move	48 挙動 Move	49 挙　動　Move
右上段外受け。左拳は引き手。 Execute a Right-Jodan-Soto-Uke. The left fist is in the Hikite position.	左中段突き。 Execute a Left-Chudan-Tsuki.	右中段突き。 Execute a Right-Chudan-Tsuki.

西
West

右真身猫足立ち。
Right-Mami-Nekoashidachi

右足を西へすり込みながら、左足を引きつけ右真身猫足立ち。

Sliding the right foot to the west, pull the left foot inward to be the Right-Mami-Nekoashidachi.

西
West

右真身猫足立ち。
Right-Mami-Nekoashidachi

そのまま。

Maintain the same position.

西
West

右真身猫足立ち。
Right-Mami-Nekoashidachi

そのまま。

Maintain the same position.

北
North

そのまま。

Maintain the same position.

[備考] 48～49挙動は連続して行う。

[Note] Execute Movements 48 and 49 continuously.

クーシャンクー

	50 挙動 Move		**51 挙動 Move**	
手の動作 Hands	右上段外受け。左拳は引き手（受けと蹴りは同時）。 Execute a Right-Jodan-Soto-Uke. The left fist is in the Hikite position. (Execute a Uke and a Keri simultaneously.)		左上段手刀受け。右手は手刀で胸前に構える。 Execute a Left-Jodan-Shuto-Uke. Hold the right hand in a Shuto in front of the chest.	左前膊を掌面下にしながら、 Place the left forearm below the palm and on the left side.
着眼点 Point to see	北 North ⑥⑦	（北から見る） Seen from the north. ⑥⑦-A	南 South ⑥⑧	南 South ⑥⑨
立ち方 Stance	左足立ち。 Stand on the left foot.	⑥⑦-A	左真半身猫足立ち。 Left-Mahanmi-Nekoashidachi	
北 North / 西 West / 東 East / 南 South				
足の動作 Feet	北へ中段右横蹴り。 Execute a Chudan-Right-Yoko-Keri to the north.		右足を左足脇へ添えておろし、左足を南側へ出し、左真半身猫足立ちとなる。 Lower the right foot to the side of the left foot, move the left foot towards the south and stand in the Left-Mahanmi-Nekoashidachi position.	左踵を付ける。 Lower the left heel to the floor.
留意点 Point	留意点 49 50 挙動 突いた位置から蹴りと同時に上段外受けを行う。 In Movements 49 and 50, from the Tsuki position, execute a Jodan-Soto-Uke while executing a Keri.		留意点 51 52 挙動 真半身猫足立ちより踵を落してから水平落し受けを行ってはならない。同時に行いながら突く。 In Movements 51 and 52, do not execute a horizontal Otoshi-Uke in the Mahanmi-Nekoashidachi position after lowering the heel. Simultaneously execute an Otoshi-Uke and push.	
動作の分解 Kumite in detail				

52 挙動 Move	53 挙動 Move	54 挙動 Move
左前膊を掌面下にして中段を落し受け、右手で貫手中段突き。	右貫手を外捻りしつつ、左拳槌で中段横打ち。右拳は引き手。	左裏拳で上段打ち。
Place the left forearm (the palm facing down), execute a Otoshi-Uke in Chudan and execute a Nukite-Chudan-Tsuki with the right hand.	Twisting a Right-Nukite outward, execute a Chudan-Yoko-Uchi with a left Kentsui. The right fist is in Hikite.	Execute a Jodan-Uchi with a Left-Ura-Ken.

南 South / 南 South / 南 South / 南 South

⑦⓪ / ⑦① / ⑦② / ⑦③

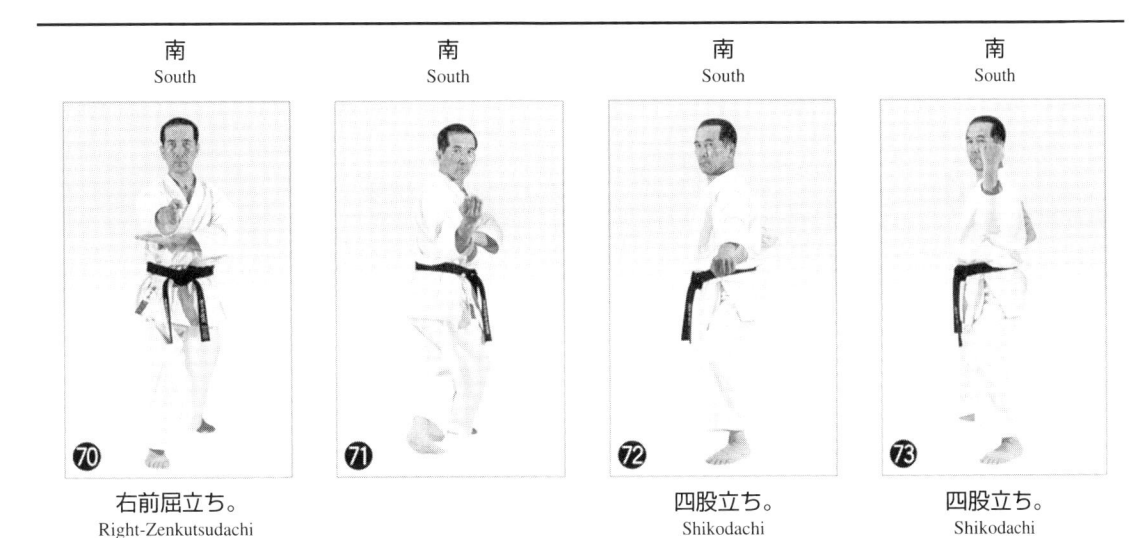

右前屈立ち。 Right-Zenkutsudachi / 四股立ち。 Shikodachi / 四股立ち。 Shikodachi

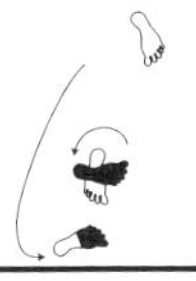

右足を南方向へ進め、右前屈立ちとなる。	前屈立ちから、右足を軸にして（⑦①）南へ左回りで四股立ちとなる（⑦②）。	四股立ちのまま南へすり込む。
Move the right foot towards the south, and stand in the Right-Zenkutsudachi position.	From Zenkutsudachi, pivoting on the right foot (⑦①), turn to the south (to the left) and stand in the Shikodachi position.	Holding the Shikodachi position, slide towards the south.

留意点 52 53 54 55 挙動　貫手の肘を脱力し腕を外捻りしながら左膝を柔らかく南に体を送り、四股立ちになると同時に拳槌打ちをする。四股立ちが不正確な場合、連続して行う技が極まらない。

In Movements 52, 53, 54 and 55, relax the Nukite elbow. Turn the arm outward and turn the body towards the south by turning the left knee and stand in a Shikodachi. At the same time execute a Kentsui-Uchi. If the Shikodachi position is unstable, continuous wazas can not be executed correctly.

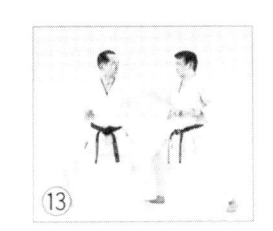

⑪ / ⑫ / ⑬ / ⑭

187

クーシャンクー

	55 挙動 Move	56 挙動 Move	57 挙動 Move
手の動作 Hands	体を左側方に向け、左拳を開手とし、横に構え、右肘に当てる。 Turn the body to the left, open the left fist. Keep the left hand in a horizontal position and move it, so it touches the right elbow.	右中段払い。左腕は垂直に立てて左上段に構える。 Execute a Right-Chudan-Harai. Raise the left arm and hold it vertically in front of and slightly above the left side of the forehead (Left-Jodan).	左腕尺骨で中段を掬い受け（肘を伸ばす）。右腕は垂直に立て、右上段に構える。 Execute a Chudan-Sukui-Uke with the side of the left elbow (extend the elbow). Raise the right arm vertically and slightly above the right side of the forehead (Right-Jodan).
着眼点 Point to see	南 South	北 North	東 East
	⓻④	⓻⑤	(北から見る) Seen from the north. ⑦⑤-A　⓻⑥
立ち方 Stance	左逆突き立ち。 Left-Gyaku-Tsukidachi	八字立ち。 Hachijidachi	四股立ち。 Shikodachi
足の動作 Feet	南へすり込みながら左逆突き立ち。 Sliding towards the south, execute a Left-Gyaku-Tsukidachi.	右足を引きながら西側へ体を開き、八字立ちとなる。 Pulling the right foot, turn the body to the west and stand in a Hachijidachi position.	右足を軸にして北側へ右回りし、四股立ちとなる。 Pivoting on the right foot, turn to the north (to the right) and stand in a Shikodachi.
留意点 Point	[備考] 53～55挙動は連続で行う。 [Note] Execute from Movement 53 to 55 continuously.	留意点 56 57挙動 肘打ちより体の捻りで右足を引き中段に払う。四股立ちになると同時に体の中心まで肘を曲げずに中段掬い受けをする。 In Movements 56 and 57, from the Hiji-Uchi, turn the body and pull then push out the right foot in a Chudan. Stand in the Shikodachi position while executing a Chudan-Sukui-Uke to the center of the body without bending the elbow.	
動作の分解 Kumite in detail	⑮	⑯	⑰

188

58 挙 動 Move	59 挙 動 Move
左腕はそのまま。右腕尺骨側で中段掬い受け（右は下）。 Hold the left arm as is. Execute a Chudan-Sukui-Uke with the right elbow bone side. (The right arm is lower.)	左右手刀にして上段受け。 Make a Shuto with right and left hand and execute a Jodan-Uke.

東
East

東
East

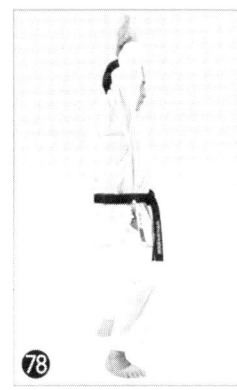

（東から見る）
Seen from the east.

⑦⑦ 　　　　　　　⑦⑧　　　　　　　⑦⑧-A

四股立ち。
Shikodachi

四股立ち。
Shikodachi

そのまま。	そのまま。
Maintain the same position.	Maintain the same position.

［備考］56〜57挙動は連続で行う。

[Note] Execute Movements 56 and 57 continuously.

⑱

189

クーシャンクー

60 挙 動　Move

手の動作 Hands	そのまま。 Maintain the same position.	そのまま。 Maintain the same position.
着眼点 Point to see	東 East	北 North
	（東から見る） Seen from the east.	（北から見る） Seen from the north.
立ち方 Stance	⑦⑨－A	⑧⓪－A　右前屈立ち。 Right-Zenkutsudachi
足の動作 Feet		右足を軸にして北へ右回りし、右前屈立ちとなる。 Pivoting on the right foot, turn to the right (to the north) and stand in a Right-Zenkutsudachi.

留意点 Point

留意点 59 60 61 挙動　手刀上段受けからの移動は北に背を向けて回ってはならない。上半身の中心軸を保ち左足の膝を柔らかく大きく運びながら北に振り向き左右の拳で中段落し受けを行う。

In Movements 59, 60 and 61, when moving the body from the Shuto-Jodan-Uke position, do not expose your back to the north. Maintain the center axis of the upper body and move the left knee wide in a flexible movement. Turn back to the north, execute a Chudan-Otoshi-Uke with the left and right fists.

動作の分解 Kumite in detail

⑲

190

61 挙　動　Move

左右を拳とし、中段落し受け（交差のまま）。

Make right and left fists. Execute a Chudan-Otoshi-Uke. (Both arms are crossed.)

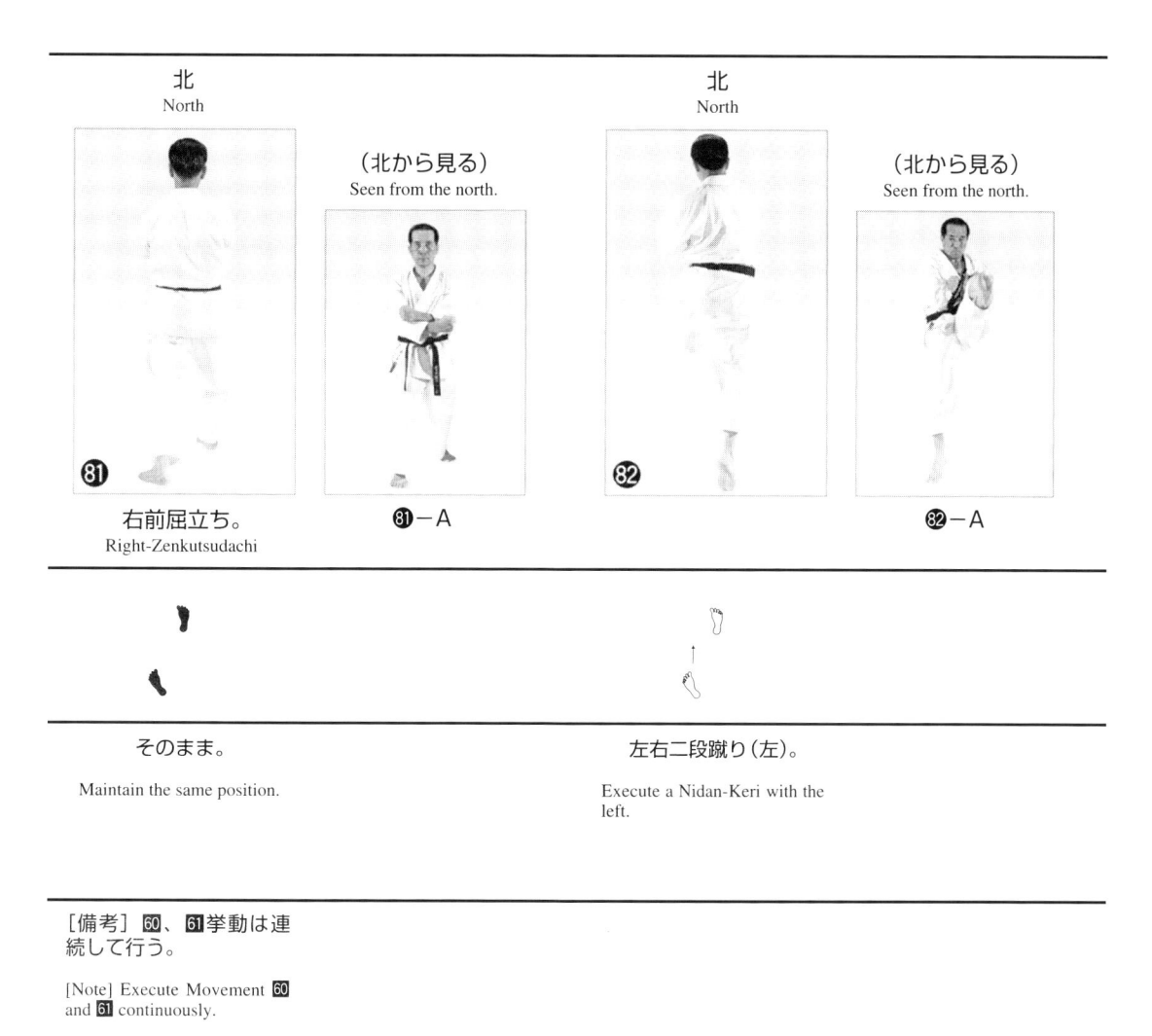

北
North

（北から見る）
Seen from the north.

⑧1

⑧1－A

右前屈立ち。
Right-Zenkutsudachi

北
North

（北から見る）
Seen from the north.

⑧2

⑧2－A

そのまま。

Maintain the same position.

左右二段蹴り（左）。

Execute a Nidan-Keri with the left.

［備考］⑩、⑪挙動は連続して行う。

[Note] Execute Movement ⑩ and ⑪ continuously.

クーシャンクー

62 挙 動 Move

手の動作 / Hands

着地と同時に右裏拳で上段打ち。

Execute a Jodan-Uchi with the right Ura-Ken while landing.

着眼点 / Point to see

北 / North

（北から見る） / Seen from the north.

㊴

㊴－A

北 / North

（北から見る） / Seen from the north.

㊱

右前屈立ち。
Right-Zenkutsudachi

㊱－A

立ち方 / Stance

北 North / 西 West / 東 East / 南 South

足の動作 / Feet

左右二段蹴り（右）。

Execute a Nidan-Keri with the right.

着地は北へ右足前に前屈立ちとなる。

Land in a north position. Placing the right foot in front, stand in the Zenkutsudachi position.

留意点 / Point

動作の分解 / Kumite in detail

63 挙動 Move

右腕撓骨側で相手の脚を掬い（⑧⑥）、左腕を右腕下に入れながら（⑧⑦）、両腕で一気に掬い上げる（⑧⑧）。

On the right arm radius side, scoop the opponent's leg (⑧⑥) and insert the left arm through the under side of the right arm (⑧⑦), then quickly scoop up the opponent's body with both arms (⑧⑧).

東 East	南 South	南 South	南 South
⑧⑤	⑧⑥	⑧⑦	⑧⑧
	四股立ち。 Shikodachi	四股立ち。 Shikodachi	

	右足を軸にして、南側へ右回りし、四股立ちとなる。	そのまま。	そのまま。
	Pivoting on the right foot, make a right turn to face south to be in Shikodachi.	Maintain the same position.	Maintain the same position.

留意点 62 63 挙動 右膝を低く屈しながら南に転じるとき、右拳は下段の掬い受けを行い、左拳は右拳に添えて一気に四股立ちの足幅で拳上する。そのとき上半身は前傾姿勢に屈しないで前方を見る。伸ばした膝の力は抜く。

In Movements 62 and 63, when lowering the right knee and turning to the south, execute a Gedan-Sukui-Uke with the right fist. Place the left fist along the right fist, and execute a Tsuki quickly and change the standing position to a Shikodachi. At that point, do not slouch the upper half of the body but keep it still, looking forward. Relax the extended knee.

⑳ ㉑

193

クーシャンクー

	止め Stop	直立 Stand
手の動作 Hands	用意の姿勢と同じ。 Same as the Ready position.	両手は開いて大腿前に軽く添える。 Open both hands and place them in front of the thighs, touching the thighs lightly.
着眼点 Point to see	南 South ⑧⑨	南 South ⑨⓪
立ち方 Stance	八字立ち。 Hachijidachi	結び立ち。 Musubidachi
足の動作 Feet	右足を戻して用意の姿勢に戻る。 Return the right foot to the original position and stand in the Ready position.	左、右と引き、結び立ちに直る。 Pull the left foot and right foot and stand in a Musubidachi.
留意点 Point		

北 North / 西 West / 東 East / 南 South

194

真半身猫足立ち手刀受け
Mahanmi-Nekoashidachi Shuto-Uke

右手刀受けより左真半身手刀受けの分解写真
Detailed pictures from Right-Shuto-Uke to Left-Mahanmi-Shuto-Uke

体の移動と共に右受け手は肘を緩め、左手刀は真っ直ぐ立てながら真身より腰は右方向に回転し真半身立ちに極めると同時に受け手・構え手が極まる。

When moving the body, relax the right elbow (Right-Ukete) and raise the left arm (Left-shuto) vertically. Turn the waist towards the right from the Mami, stand in the Mahanmidachi. At the same time execute an Ukete and Kamaete.

中央技術委員会　教範作成小委員会

荒川　　通	TORU ARAKAWA
栗原　茂夫	SHIGEO KURIHARA
塩見　　明	AKIRA SHIOMI
村田　　寛	HIROSHI MURATA
津山　捷泰	KATSUHIRO TSUYAMA
坂上　節明	SADAAKI SAKAGAMI
伊藤　洋造	YOZO ITO

演武者

前田　利明	TOSHIAKI MAEDA
大坂　可治	YOSHIHARU OSAKA
佐々木清巳	KIYOMI SASAKI
古川　哲也	TETSUYA FURUKAWA
長谷川行光	YUKIMITSU HASEGAWA
大島　　望	NOZOMI OSHIMA

演武補助

長谷川克英	KATSUHIDE HASEGAWA
野崎　　宏	HIROSHI NOZAKI
金井　孔明	KOMEI KANAI
根本　敬介	KEISUKE NEMOTO

第2指定形　空手道形教範

2013年12月17日改定版第一刷
2018年5月1日改定版第二刷

編集　　公益財団法人全日本空手道連盟　中央技術委員会
編者　　公益財団法人全日本空手道連盟
発行　　株式会社チャンプ
　　　　〒166-0003　東京都杉並区高円寺南4-19-3　総和第二ビル
　　　　電話：03-3315-3190（営業部）

©Japan Karatedo Federation 2013
Printed in Japan　　印刷：シナノ印刷株式会社

定価はカバーに表示してあります。